LIGHT ON THE FOUR GOSPELS FROM THE SINAI PALIMPSEST

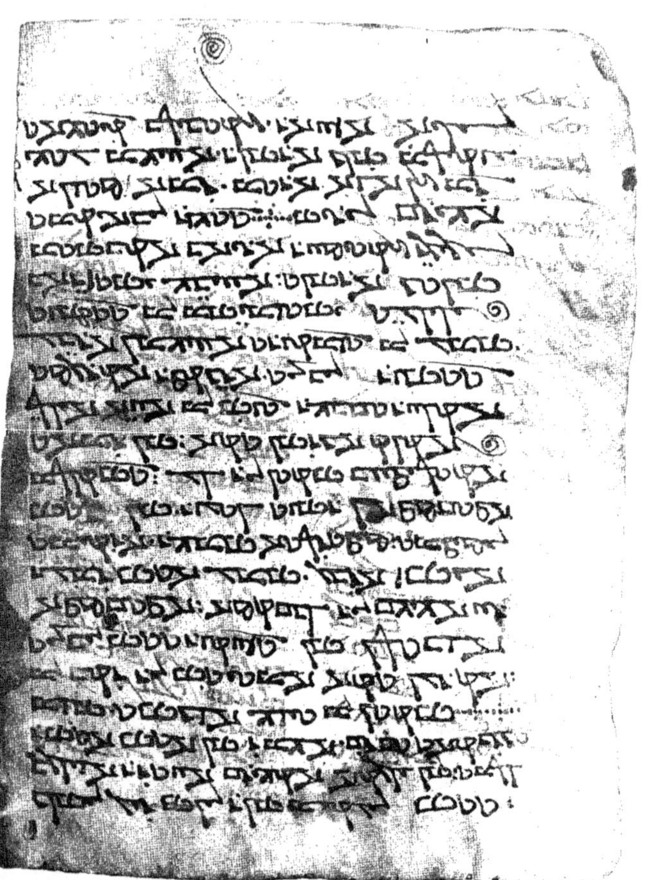

Folio 29a

Script. inf., Luke xx. 33-44. Script sup. (*reversed*), Acts of Eugenia.

[*Frontispiece.*

LIGHT ON THE FOUR GOSPELS FROM THE SINAI PALIMPSEST

BY

AGNES SMITH LEWIS

Hon. D.D. (Heidelberg), Ph.D. (Halle), LL.D. (St Andrews), Litt.D. (Dublin), F.N.B.A.

Wipf & Stock
PUBLISHERS
Eugene, Oregon

Wipf and Stock Publishers
199 W 8th Ave, Suite 3
Eugene, OR 97401

Light on the Four Gospels from the Sinai Palimpsest
By Lewis, Agnes Smith
ISBN: 1-59752-285-6
Publication date 7/1/2005
Previously published by Williams & Norgate, 1913

TO

REV. CANON ROBERT HATCH KENNETT, D.D.

REGIUS PROFESSOR OF HEBREW IN THE UNIVERSITY OF CAMBRIDGE

AND

JAMES RENDEL HARRIS, LITT.D., LL.D.

DIRECTOR OF STUDIES AT WOODBROOKE SETTLEMENT, BIRMINGHAM

THIS BOOK IS DEDICATED
IN GRATEFUL REMEMBRANCE OF THEIR KIND INSTRUCTION
IN THE SYRIAC TONGUE, IN PALÆOGRAPHY, AND
OTHER ARTS, WITHOUT WHICH IT COULD
NOT HAVE BEEN WRITTEN

PREFACE

This little book has been written at the suggestion of some young friends, theological students at Westminster College, Cambridge, who thought that the substance of a lecture which I gave them a few years ago might be made interesting to a wider public. I have tried to avoid those technicalities which often repel even people of high intelligence from the reading of a serious book, wherever I could do so without making my meaning obscure. Every reader of the English Bible has the right to know all he can about it. My remarks are not intended for those who are acquainted with Greek or with Syriac ; and if this work should fall into their hands, I trust that they will forgive its many omissions, and reflect that the way is open to them to search for furthur information in more scientific books. Those who wish to read my translation of the Sinai text may obtain it from Messrs Clay & Sons, of the Cambridge University Press Warehouse, Ave Maria Lane, London.

The page which I have chosen from 362 others for the illustration, exhibits as its first word, nay, as its first letter, one of those minute points in which my reading of the Syriac text differs from Dr Burkitt's. Its upper script is turned upside down.

My thanks are specially due to my twin-sister, Dr Margaret Dunlop Gibson, for help in the reading of my proof-sheets; and to the Rev. James Hastings, D.D., for his permission to use matter which has already appeared in the *Expository Times*.

AGNES SMITH LEWIS.

CASTLE-BRAE,
CAMBRIDGE, *October* 1913.

CONTENTS

Light on the Four Gospels from the Sinai Palimpsest

CHAPTER I

PRELIMINARY

THE publication of the Syriac text of the Gospels from the Sinai Palimpsest in October 1894, has given rise to fresh discussions with regard to more than one interesting problem connected with the birth and life of our Lord, and especially with the mystery of the Incarnation. I wish to offer a few suggestions about these, and also about the position which the version represented by the Sinai Palimpsest, and which, for want of a better term, I shall continue to call the Old Syriac, occupies in relation to the text represented in the earliest Greek MSS.; the text which, from its age-long acceptance by the Christian Church, has a first claim to the title of Orthodox. I am aware that the fact of my having been the discoverer of the chief, because the oldest and most perfect known representative of this version, gives me no special insight into the question; and anything which I have to advance about it can be only a theory. Yet, if that theory be wrong, it seems to me that success in the search for truth is frequently like success in the art of photography: we advance to a sure knowledge of our subject in spite of our mistakes, and sometimes even by means of them.

Two chief theories have been in vogue to account for the general agreement of the Synoptic Gospels; some of our Lord's discourses and parables being reported by their authors in nearly identical words, although the chronological arrangement and the structure of their respective narratives vary so greatly. The theory of oral transmission has been almost bowled out of the field by that of an original Gospel, from which the Evangelists Matthew, Mark, and Luke all in their turn borrowed.

But is the oral theory so unreasonable? This is surely a case where the probabilities of human conduct must be taken into account. The immediate followers of our Lord were not bookmen, still less were they scholars. They were, like most Oriental peasants, in close touch with their fellow-men, and with the life of the synagogue, of the city-gate, and of the bazaar. Let us try to imagine how such people would act, when placed in circumstances of unique, nay, of transcendent importance. If we could transport ourselves to that upper room in Jerusalem, where, day by day, the disciples watched for the coming of the Holy Ghost, in suppressed but ecstatic rapture over the recollection of their Risen Master; or if we could follow them for long months after Pentecost, within the doors of their meeting-places, what should we hear? No formal reading from the Law or the Prophets, surely, no set prayers nor liturgy, but a pouring into each other's ears of what each could recollect, whether of our Lord's actions, His parables, His discourses, and even of His outward mien.

One and another would supply details; one would pick up some dropped phrase, to which the other would assent; and these stories would be repeated, improved upon, or revised, till at last, each of them fell into an approved form, which those who had the best memory or the most acceptable gift of speech would be called upon to relate. The necessity for committing this to parchment did not become evident immediately, and thus the Gospels are said to have been composed at a later date than any of the Epistles. The wants of posterity were held of little account by men who expected their Master's second advent to take place during their own lifetime. But when some of the Apostles died, and then some of the older disciples; when children were born who had to be taught to realise what they had never seen; and when the community was scattered by persecution—then, as Luke tells us, many took in hand to set in order a declaration of those things which were most surely believed by all.

That this was done in Greek by three out of the four Evangelists has long been an accepted tradition; though it is now on philological evidence disputed. Papias reported that St Matthew wrote his Gospel in Aramaic, and, if so, it is hard to believe that one of the Syriac versions, which has come down to us, does not give us, to a large extent, some of his original expressions.

These Greek Gospels, no doubt, embodied much of what had been already stereotyped in oral form. Hence the frequently verbal agreement of the Synoptics. Being the undoubted work of the Evangelists, one of whom, Matthew, was an Apostle, and being written in the popular Greek language of the day, they were at once accepted by the Greek-speaking section of the Church, whose metropolis at that time was Antioch.

Is there any improbability in supposing that these Greek Gospels were translated into Syriac, the vernacular of Palestine, very soon after their promulgation? The labour of making many copies must have employed many hands; and the Semitic natives of the country, most of whom were unacquainted with Greek, or who had a knowledge of it sufficient only for commercial purposes, would demand at a very early period a version in their own tongue. Is it not possible that this version (from Greek into Syriac) was made by men who had either been themselves eye-witnesses of the events recorded, or in whose ears were still ringing certain phrases or expressions heard by them in the synagogue from the lips of those who had been eye-witnesses? If this were so, they would, whilst giving in general a faithful rendering of the Greek text before them, occasionally and naturally fall into the habit of incorporating with it, or modifying it so as to incorporate, those phrases or expressions with which they had acquired a sacred familiarity. And the result would be just what we have in the Old Syriac Gospels, and in the Western texts generally.

This, of course, presupposes an older date for the Sinaitic text than that of Tatian's Diatessaron (A.D. 160). Should it be proved, beyond the shadow of a doubt, that the Diatessaron came first, I frankly admit that my theory would be baseless. Yet I cannot imagine how a body of Christians, in the first fervour of their faith in the Risen Saviour, could have been content to wait till A.D. 160 for a version of the New Testament. And my supposition will at least account for the curious circumstance, that the Old Syriac Version is extant only in the Gospels. The Peshiṭta or Syriac Vulgate is supposed to be a revision of this Old Syriac text, made by Rabbula, Bishop of Edessa, about A.D. 415. It comprises the Gospels, the Pauline and the Catholic Epistles; whilst the Philoxenian and the Harcleian include, with these, the four shorter Apostolic ones. And in the case of the Palestinian Syriac, or Galilean, not only have fragments of the Pauline Epistles been discovered by Dr Land, Dr Rendel Harris, myself, and others, but considerable portions of these, in a consecutive text, are in a palimpsest manuscript now in my own possession, which I have called *Codex Climaci Rescriptus*. In the Old Syriac not a word of the Epistles has been seen anywhere; or, if seen, it has not been clearly differentiated from the text of the Peshiṭta. A quotation from the Acts, which is supposed to be Old Syriac, has been found in Aphraates; but the Acts is a history; and a version of it might be affected by the same causes as those that have given us variants in the Gospels. I am thus assuming that the text of the old Greek MSS., as represented substantially in the works of Griesbach, Lachman, Tischendorf, Tregelles, Scrivener, Westcott and Hort, Nestle, and others of those eminent scholars whose labours have paved the way for our Revised Version, has the first claim to our veneration. But it may at the same time be conceded that the Syriac MSS. give us, in their remarkable divergences from the received text, a true echo of what was in the minds of some of the early disciples, as having fallen from the lips of their Master.

I grant that this is to claim a very high antiquity for the Old Syriac Version. But is there any certain reason for pronouncing it absolutely impossible? It seems to have become a maxim of safe—I will not say sound

—criticism to fix the date of a document at the very latest period which the facts will warrant. Does this exclude the possibility, when we are in the realm of conjecture, of a much earlier date being the true one?

Those who wish to see how the argument for the priority of the Sinai Version over the Diatessaron is strengthened by a number of minute details should study Dr Hjelt's book, *Die Altsyrische Evangelienübersetzung*, for themselves.

His theory offers the one satisfactory explanation of a circumstance which has long puzzled me. Why is the conclusion which has been added to St Mark's Gospel, *i.e.* chap. xvi. vv. 9–20, absent in the Sinai Version and present in the Curetonian? for chap. xvi. vv. 17–20 is the only portion of Mark which we possess in the latter. The answer is, "Because Tatian came between them." Tatian copied that conclusion from some of the Greek MSS. which he used in addition to the Old Syriac, and the translator (or editor) of the Curetonian followed him.

It has been suggested, with some plausibility, that the Syriac MSS. and the Old Latin ones, which have a close resemblance to them, are merely incorrect copies of the Sacred Autograph, and were as such rejected by the Church when the Canon of the New Testament was fixed.

It may be so, but I would urge that there are in the Sinai Palimpsest some remarkable readings, which are more in harmony with their context than those of similar passages hitherto known. In citing these, I must explain that they are taken not only from the major portion of the text as transcribed in 1893 by Professor Bensly, Dr Rendel Harris, and Dr Burkitt, but also from the minor portion which my third visit to Sinai in 1895 enabled me to add to it.

The greater conciseness of the Sinai text in John xvi. 28, where the phrase, "I leave the world," is omitted, and in John xvii., where "even as I am not of it" (*i.e.* the world), occurs in ver. 16 only (not in ver. 14), might even be held to indicate that the text from which it is translated is an earlier one than the Sinaiticus, the Vaticanus, or the Alexandrinus.

But, side by side with those instances of conciseness, and with those which commend themselves by their appropriateness, such as Mark x. 50, xvi. 3; Luke i. 64; John xii. 31, we have in the same codex variations which, if they are not corruptions, can only be explained on the supposition that our Lord repeated His parables and portions of His dis-discourses more than once to different audiences. We see no inherent improbability in this, when we consider that our short Gospels chronicle the events and teachings of a three years' active ministry. Of these we have assuredly no *verbatim* report, but one made several years later, from memory.

CHAPTER II

CAUSES OF VARIANTS

THE age which accepted the theory of verbal inspiration has passed away. It was a comfortable and convenient theory, but it received its death-blow in England at last from the Revised Version of the Bible. No one who has ever read two out of the 3829 extant MSS. and fragments of the New Testament, or even two of their printed texts, and has observed the many slight variations in the order of their words, and sometimes even in the words themselves, can continue to hold this theory for a single moment.

We must recollect that before the Four Gospels came to us, copies of them were multiplied during 1500 years by the hands and the brains of fallible men. No special

Providence watched over the scribes ; and the miracle is, that in spite of vagaries in spelling, and of occasional diversities of diction, the substantial agreement among these MSS. should be so great and so preponderating as it is.

Dr Hort has estimated that, though 30,000 variants have been counted in the New Testament, seven-eighths of its text are in no way affected by them. Those that are not due to orthography (that is, spelling) amount to one-sixtieth of the whole text. Substantial variants amount to about one word in a thousand.

The causes of these variants are not far to seek. Any honest printer would smile at the ignorance of an author who expected him to have no mistakes in a first impression, even of a concert programme. And the copying of Gospel MSS. was, in the early centuries, sometimes done under circumstances which were very far removed, I will not say from the quiet, but certainly from the method and regularity, of a modern printing-office.

Moreover, most of these variants occur in the least important parts of the Gospel narrative, in the connecting-links between its weighty sentences. For instance, the phrase, "Jesus answered and said unto him," may be put in at least thirteen different ways :—

Jesus answered, and said unto him,
Jesus answering, said unto him,
Jesus answered him, saying,
Jesus said unto him,
Jesus answered, saying,
Jesus answering, said,
And Jesus said unto him,
And Jesus said,
Jesus said,
Jesus answered, and said,
And Jesus answering, said unto him,
And Jesus answered him, saying,
And Jesus answered, saying.

In Greek, we can place the verb before its subject, "Answered Jesus and said unto him." Or we can prefix an adverb to the phrase, "Then Jesus answered," etc. Take two different MSS., say the Codex Sinaiticus and the Codex Bezæ, and if in one place—Matt. xi. 4, for instance—you do not find a perfect verbal agreement in this phrase, it will be counted as a variant. In Greek also, you can begin it with "Ἀποκριθεὶς δὲ" or with "καὶ ἀποκριθεὶς." The man who would allow his faith in the Gospels to be shaken by such a trifle has never comprehended God's ways of working in the realm of Nature.

Why, we may ask, has God allowed these variants to exist? Why has He not made the very copyists of His Word infallible? Our answer is, Look at His plans in other departments where we are concerned. We are fellow-workers with Him in the humble sphere of feeding and clothing ourselves. God provides the corn, but man has to sow and reap, grind and cook, before it becomes fit for his sustenance. God gives us the sheep's fleece, and the down of the cotton-plant, but how many human hands must work on them before they are turned into well-fitting garments? Henry Drummond, in his *Ascent of Man*, pp. 257–266 *seqq.*, points out that man becomes a nobler animal through the effort to supply his own bodily wants. So God, having provided us with the Revelation of His truth which is contained in the Scriptures of the Old and New Testaments (so saith the Westminster Assembly's Shorter Catechism, compiled in A.D. 1648), left to His human prophets perfect freedom to use their own words in delivering His message, and to human scribes to embody their own ideas of accuracy in copying it. Have the latter been faithful?

It is the same with them as with all who use God's other gifts. He gives us pure water, rising from the earth in mountain-springs, but is it pure when it reaches the cities? Or when it has passed through them?

And He has given us the institution of marriage, which was designed for our comfort, and, when properly observed, is an untold blessing to ourselves and to the generations that shall follow us. But human perversity has exceeded itself in its manifold methods for spoiling this divine arrangement. The many marriages which are contracted from unworthy motives, resulting in grievous suffering to both parties; the tales, not entirely fictitious, which we read in modern novels, in the records of the Divorce Courts, or those which our own experience of life has led us to observe, tell with a thousand tongues of how man has marred God's plan for his welfare.

We are called to be fellow-workers with Him also in the transmission of His Word. He makes even our mistakes, and those of our fellow-men, to praise Him, for the very variants which frighten the weak-minded amongst us act as a stimulant to others, inciting them to search the Scriptures more diligently, to eliminate the mistakes of mere copyists, and to ascertain what it was that the Evangelists actually wrote. Thus it was that the seed of the Word sprouted anew, so to speak, in the sixteenth century; and thus it has been throughout the whole of the nineteenth century; till at length a company of scholars met in the Jerusalem Chamber at Westminster, and gave us the Revised Version of our English Bible.

Has that Version given us the last word? We trow not; for when any good thing becomes stereotyped, it ceases to grow. And growth is a law of life.

We can never forget how our Revisers have revealed to us the original beauty of many passages in God's Word. For instance, the passage in Isa. viii. 21–ix. 7. And in the New Testament, their restoration of "love" in the thirteenth chapter of 1 Corinthians is an outstanding example. "Charity = caritas" is an artificial word, coined by St Jerome because of the poverty of the Latin language, which could not distinguish between ἀγάπη and ἔρως, between the disinterested love of friends and the love of sweethearts. But "charity" is a very inappropriate term for the expression of our feelings towards God; especially as we often use it in the sense of "almsgiving" or of "forbearance." The love which the Apostle Paul desired so greatly for himself and for his spiritual children has God for its first object; and man, the child of God, for its secondary one. Charity, in such a connection, is simply absurd.

The object of this little book is not to

depreciate the work of the Revisers. They have accomplished a great task, in which learning, skill, ingenuity, and patience were alike required. But, as I have said, "growth is a principle of life," and before the last of these distinguished men had passed away, new light has been shed on the subject of their labours, from sources to which they had not complete access: chiefly from the early Syriac and Latin Versions, from the Greek cursives, and from the Oxyrhynchus papyri.

I am induced to write about the Old Syriac Version chiefly because it has been suggested to me by some of my young friends, who are preparing for the Christian ministry, that I ought to gather into a small compass the chief characteristics of the ancient text which I had the happiness of discovering in the library of St Catherine's Monastery on Mount Sinai in the year 1892, which my twin-sister, Mrs Margaret Dunlop Gibson, helped me at that time to photograph in its entirety; and whose text was first identified, at my request, as being similar to that of the Curetonian manuscript, by the late Dr Bensly and by Professor Burkitt. It was transcribed in 1893 by these two gentlemen, and by Dr Rendel Harris (whose good advice had prepared me for its discovery), to the extent of about four-fifths; while most of the remaining fifth, which one of these original transcribers considered illegible, was deciphered by me in 1895, and supplemented during three subsequent visits which my sister and I made to the monastery in 1897, 1902, and 1906.

No one therefore can know better than myself what the text of the palimpsest manuscript really is—not even Professor Burkitt, who has tacked its variants, including nearly the whole Gospel of St Mark, to his new edition of the Curetonian Syriac Gospels. Why, it may be asked, should the text of a Syriac manuscript, which is confessedly a translation, and not the original, be considered of so much importance by scholars? Their opinion of its value has increased rather than diminished, as the years have gone by since its first publication in 1894.

One reason is because of the language in which it is written. Syriac or rather Christian Aramaic was undoubtedly the mother-tongue of our Lord the Christ. We know this from the few Syriac phrases which are incorporated in the Greek text, instead of being translated, such as "Talitha cumi" ("Maiden, arise"); "Ethphatha"[1] ("Be opened"); and, above all, by His dying words on the Cross, "Eli Eli, lama sabaqthani" ("My God, my God, why hast thou forsaken me?"). It is worth noting that these words were spoken in the Galilean dialect of Aramaic which bewrayed St Peter, a dialect which bore the same relation to the literary or Edessene Syriac as Doric to Attic, or as Scotch to English. There are not many MSS. of this dialect extant; the oldest one being a palimpsest, chiefly of St Paul's Epistles, *in a continuous text*, not broken up into Lessons, which has been assigned by the chief Semitic authorities in the British Museum to the sixth century, and is now my property.

If our Lord had spoken Edessene Syriac in

[1] Greek, Ephphatha.

that supreme moment of His sufferings, He would have said "lemana shabaqthani" instead of "lama sabaqthani." And I cannot help wondering if He would have said "sibboleth" instead of "shibboleth" if He had lived in the days of Jephthah. The first specimen of spoken Aramaic which we find in the Bible is in Gen. xxxi. 47. There we are told that when Jacob and Laban had set up a heap of stones as a witness between them, Jacob called it in Hebrew, "Galeed," "the heap of witness," and Laban called it "Jegar-sahadutha," which means the same thing in Aramaic. This shows that Aramaic was the language spoken in Charan, where Laban dwelt.

A tongue akin to Aramaic is largely used in the cuneiform script of Assyria and Babylonia. It must therefore be very ancient. Throughout the Old Testament, the country north of Palestine is always called Aram; its people were the Aramæans, and their language was Aramaic. But when they became Christians, finding that they were often mistaken for Armaians, *i.e.* heathen, they allowed their land to be called by its Greek name of Syria, themselves to be christened Syrians, and their speech Syriac.

The children of Judah who returned from Babylon in the time of Cyrus brought the Babylonian Aramaic with them, the very tongue which Abraham had spoken in Ur and in Charan. The common people had then forgotten Hebrew, so that Ezra and other scribes had to translate the Law to them, as well as to expound it. This continued until our Lord's time, for we find that all proper names in the New Testament, where they are not Greek, are Syriac; such as Sapphira, "the beautiful one"; Cephas, "a stone"; and all names beginning with "Bar," "the son of," equivalent to the Hebrew "Ben," or the Celtic "Mac."

The second reason lies in the purity of its text. The Sinai Gospels have lain in the recesses of a lonely monastery, unread for at least 1200 years, since the day when John the Stylite, of Beth-Mari Caddish, at a place called Ma'rrath Meṣrin, near Antioch on the Orontes, covered them over with a second writing—a collection of biographies of Holy Women.

The doings of these remarkable, but rather frisky saints, form very instructive reading ; so we cannot wonder that in the year A.D. 697 or 778 John the Stylite took an old volume of the Gospels and used it as writing-material on which to record the adventures of these ladies. The papyrus-plant had then been all used up ; paper was waiting to be invented by the Chinese, a century later ; and vellum must have been very scarce in a desert monastery. It seems to us almost miraculous that a translation of the Four Gospels, made in the second century, and copied, probably, in the fourth one, should, when deciphered and released (as Dr Rendel Harris puts it) "from its palimpsest prison," *i.e.* from behind the bars of its superimposed writing, show such a great amount of agreement with the English Authorised Version. In no particular is this agreement more striking than in the many phrases of the *Textus Receptus* which are omitted by the Revisers. Every passage once familiar to our fathers, which our nineteenth-century Revisers, or Drs Westcott and Hort, have agreed to omit, are in this fourth-century manuscript conspicuous by their absence. The longest of these are Mark xvi. 9–20 and John vii. 53–viii. 11. The first of these can hardly have been written by St Mark, for the simple reason that any author who cared for his own credit would have fitted the 9th verse of chap. xvi. on to the broken 8th verse in a better style; and would not have finished a sentence with the word γὰρ, "for." St Paul, it is true, has furnished us with a phrase ending in γάρ (Phil. i. 18), but that is an interrogative sentence; and any of our Cambridge students who may do it will never be in Class I. of the Classical Tripos. Mr F. C. Conybeare, of Oxford, in the year 1891 made the very interesting discovery of an Armenian MS. at Edschmiatzin, where these twelve verses were written as a separate section, and to them was attached the name of their probable author, Ariston the Presbyter, whom some identify with Aristion, the Presbyter named by Papias in Eusebius' History.

It would hardly be safe to say, however, that

these two long passages are not part of the Gospel. To those who think, with me, that the Synoptic narratives are none of them the product of a single mind; and that none of the inspired editors whose names they bear can have actually copied from one another's writings, it is easy to believe that Mark xvi. 9–20 and John vii. 53–viii. 11 may not be the work of the Evangelists to whose Gospels they are now attached, and may yet be perfectly true records.

CHAPTER III

THE GENEALOGIES AND THE VIRGIN-BIRTH

THE genealogy of Joseph, with which the Gospel of Matthew begins, presents us with the same serious difficulties in both Greek and Syriac MSS.

It consists of three parts, each containing fourteen verses. Yet, in the second part, *i.e.* from David to Jechonia, we know from 2 Kings that there were seventeen, not fourteen generations; and that ver. 8 reads, *Joram begat Ozias.* Here the names of three of these kings are omitted, for Ahaziah, Joash, and Amaziah really came between Joram and Uzziah or Azariah, as he is called in the Old Testament. Why is Jehoram credited with being the immediate father of his own great-great-grandson? To explain this, I must bring forward a view which has come to us from Hilary[1] and Jerome,[2] and has lately been advocated by Dr J. M. Heer.

The Jewish nation is not the only one which has practised what is called the *damnatio memoriæ*, that is, the blotting out of a hated name from all public records and even inscriptions on stone. Instances of this will be found in the histories of Amen-hotep, the so-called "heretic" king of Egypt, who transported his capital from Memphis to Tel-el-Amarna in B.C. 1450; of Philip V. of Macedon, of Alcibiades, of Commodus, and others. References to it occur frequently in the Old Testament, in passages such as Exod. xxxii. 33, "Whosoever hath sinned against Me, him will I blot out of My book"; also in Deut. ix. 14, xxv. 19, xxix. 20; 2 Kings xiv. 27; Ps. ix. 5, "Thou hast destroyed the wicked, Thou hast blotted out their name for ever and ever"; Ps. lxix. 28, "Let them be blotted out of the Book of Life."

[1] See Minge's *Patrologia*, vol. ix., Comm. on Matt. i. 8.

[2] Migne, vol. xxv.; Jerome, vol. vii., c. 10, Comm. on Matthew.

And in the New Testament, Rev. iii. 5, "I will in no wise blot out his name out of the Book of Life."

These three kings, Ahaziah, Joash, and Amaziah, were not worse than others of their line; Joash, indeed, was better than some of the other Jewish monarchs. But they were all descendants of the wicked Ahab unto the fourth generation, through Athaliah, Ahab's daughter, wife of King Jehoram; and not only had a curse been pronounced on the progeny of Ahab, but he had broken the second commandment, the one of the Ten Words to which a special curse upon those who defied it was attached. In other words, he had promoted and fostered idolatry. Matthew made no mistake in omitting these three kings, for that had been done, some centuries earlier, by the priests who were the official guardians of the Temple records.

For evidence of the care with which Jewish family records were kept, we need only refer to the lists in Genesis, Samuel, Chronicles, Ruth, and Nehemiah; also to the papyri lately discovered by Dr Rubensohn in the island of Elephantine, just below the first cataract of the Nile. Though we are told by Julius Africanus (in Eusebius, *H.E.* i. 7) that Herod the Great caused most of the registers to be burnt, in order to hide from the Roman Emperor the fact that he was not himself in the line of Jewish kings; there is little doubt that these would soon be replaced from memory by those who could trace their own descent either from Aaron or from David, or probably from registers kept in private families.

In ver. 12 we read, *And after they were brought to Babylon, Jechonia begat Shealtiel, and Shealtiel begat Zerubbabel.*

This is the Jechonia, of whom it is said in Jer. xxii. 30, *Write ye this man childless.*

It is quite legitimate to suppose that Jechonia was childless, because the sons whose names we find in 1 Chron. iii. 17, 18 died young, and not because they were never born to him. The chronicler, in fact, makes Pedaiah, brother of Shealtiel, the father of Zerubbabel; and there is no inconsistency in this, because by the law of a Levirite marriage, Shealtiel might marry the widow of the childless Pedaiah, or even if Pedaiah married the widow of the childless Shealtiel, her son Zerubbabel might be reckoned to either of them. Whatever be the reason of it, Zerubbabel is more than once called the son of Shealtiel in the Book of Ezra.

It cannot be affirmed, then, that Matthew has made a mistake in either of these passages. He doubtless wrote exactly what was in the Temple register. Generations before Matthew was born, the priests had expunged the names of Ahab's descendants, through his daughter Athaliah, to the fourth generation; and since the time of Ezra, Zerubbabel had, even in his own lifetime, been called the son of Shealtiel.

Dr Heer has pointed out that the genealogy of Joseph in Matthew's Gospel is cast in exactly the same mould as the very short one which concludes the Book of Ruth. It is probable that this was the customary form for such documents; and if any change had been made in the entry, which was probably dictated by

Joseph, regarding our Lord's birth, the consequence to Mary would have been terrible. She would probably have been put to death by stoning. So we must not wonder that the Sinai text reads (ver. 16), *Joseph, to whom was betrothed Mary the Virgin, begat Jesus, who is called the Christ.*

The phrase which qualifies this statement of Joseph's paternity is probably an addition by Matthew himself to the statement which he found in the official register. For the descendants of Levi and for those of David, as the Sinai text affirms both Joseph and Mary to have been, such registering was imperative. The verse has been so much and so variously modified, both in the Curetonian MS. and in the Greek ones, that the shock of surprise which was felt both in the Unitarian camp and in the Orthodox one, at once gave rise to a charge of heresy. This charge, happily, could not be substantiated, for after the publication of the full text it was seen that not only is ver. 16 self-contradictory, but the story of the Annunciation, which begins in ver. 21, is substantially the same as it is in all Greek MSS. The only contradictory point in the narrative is in ver. 21, *She shall bear to thee a son*, and in ver. 25, *And she bore to him a son*. As, however, these phrases are found also in the Apocryphal book called the *Protevangelium Jacobii* in its Syriac version, a seventh-century palimpsest belonging to myself, whose text has been published by me as No. XI., *Studia Sinaitica*, they cannot have the significance, to Semitic minds, which we Westerns would naturally attribute to them. The chief purpose of the *Protevangelium* is to inculcate a belief in the perpetual virginity of our Lord's mother, and from its fables the whole worship of the Virgin in the Roman and probably in the Greek Church has sprung. Though it was condemned in the sixth century by Pope Gelasius in the Decretum Gelasii—a decree which has never been repealed,—Romanist writers frequently use its stories, like weapons from a rich armoury, to defend their otherwise unproved assertions about the incidents in Mary's life.

Joseph, from a legal point of view only, was the father of our Lord. In modern Arabia, as in ancient Babylon, a man is considered the father of a widow's young children if he marries her. They no longer bélong to the tribe of their real father, but to that of their stepfather. The reason for this is obvious; for we know that the strength of a clan must have been measured by the number of its men who could fight. Canon Girdlestone brought to my notice, that one of the laws in the famous Code of Hammu-rabbi, king of Babylon, *circa* B.C. 2200, is to the effect that if a man has adopted a boy as his son, that boy becomes doubly his if he teaches him a handicraft. And there can be no reasonable doubt that Jesus learnt the art of carpentering in Joseph's workshop. It was no fine art, such as that of a modern cabinet-maker; for Eastern people, when left quite to themselves, do not fill their houses with pretty furniture. An early tradition says that the articles which came out of Joseph's workshop were chiefly plough-handles, made of very perishable wood; and for that reason, no specimen of our Lord's handiwork was preserved by His disciples.

Joseph was indeed a model husband. Though it is evident from ver. 19 that he at first suspected Mary of infidelity to him, when he had been made aware by divine revelation that his suspicion was groundless, he at once threw the mantle of his protection over her.

And the Syriac versions bring out, more clearly than the Greek original, what was her true position in regard to him. In the Old Syriac and in the Peshiṭta alike, we are told that she was betrothed to him at the time of the Annunciation (Luke i. 27). She was still only betrothed at the time of her visit to Elizabeth; for, after its completion (possibly after she had been present at the circumcision of Elizabeth's son), she returned to her own house (Luke i. 56); but when she accompanied Joseph to Bethlehem, *she had the status of his wife*; for otherwise, she would have committed an outrage on all Eastern ideas of propriety by accompanying him. Thus it came to pass that our Lord was born in wedlock; and that the journey to Beth Leḥem, followed by the flight to Egypt, and a two years' residence there, saved Mary from becoming the object of gossip and perhaps of slander from the people of Nazareth, who would have been astonished at her return, so shortly after her marriage, with a baby. Considerations of this kind probably determined Mary to undertake the journey to Beth Leḥem. The Syriac versions, as we have said, leave us in no doubt about her position, for in Luke ii. 5 they call her Joseph's *wife*—no ambiguous word, such as μεμνηστευμένῃ, "espoused," or μεμνηστευμένῃ γυναικί, "espoused wife," being used. I cannot help thinking that our English Revisers were not well advised when they rendered this phrase, "who was betrothed to him." They have here followed too closely the reading of two ancient MSS.—the Sinaiticus (א) and the Vaticanus (B)—without considering the terrible consequences which must have resulted to Mary if at that time she had been only betrothed. Codex Alexandrinus (A), five of the old Latin MSS., and our Authorised Version give the much more sensible phrase, "his betrothed wife." Both the Old Syriac and the Peshiṭta have "wife" only.

Whence, then, arises the reading of the Sinai Palimpsest in Matt. i. 16, *Joseph, to whom being betrothed Mary the Virgin, begat Jesus, who is called the Christ?*

Several scholars have pointed out that we have an almost similar reading in a family of Greek cursive MSS., called the Ferrar Group, or *fam.* 13, after a learned scholar who first pointed out their relationship to each other. The ancestor of that family, from which all of them have been copied, must have had Ἰάκωβ δὲ ἐγέννησε τὸν Ἰωσήφ, ᾧ μνηστευθεῖσα παρθένος Μαριὰμ ἐγέννησεν Ἰησοῦν, τὸν λεγόμενον Χριστόν. *And Jacob begat Joseph, to whom being betrothed Mary the Virgin, begat Jesus, who is called the Christ.*

Now if you repeat "Joseph," that is, if you say, "And Jacob begat Joseph, Joseph, to whom was betrothed Mary the Virgin, begat Jesus, who is called the Christ," you have the very reading of the Sinai Palimpsest.

This reading, then, is no isolated phenomenon,

but a material link in the transmission of the Gospel text. It has been modified in various ways, to bring it into harmony with the story of the Annunciation, which follows it. And it contains a contradiction within itself. Without, however, trying to trace its descent from any other MS., I would submit to the judgment of my readers a very simple explanation. It is to be found in ver. 18, which ought in English to begin with "But."

But the birth of the Christ was on this wise. When as His mother was espoused to Joseph, before they came together, she was found with child of the Holy Ghost. "But" is a disjunctive conjunction, which always refers to a statement going before it, and it seems to me that the statement in this case, which was to be modified, was in ver. 16. As the Translators of our Authorised Version had no Old Syriac text before them, and only an altered form of ver. 16, they could not see what the "But" referred to, and they got out of the difficulty by turning "But" into "Now." And δέ used between the article in the genitive, and a noun in the genitive, does naturally mean "But." It is so translated in the Authorised Version in Matt. i. 20, ii. 19, 22, and in 162 other passages of the same Gospel. Perhaps for this reason, perhaps for others, the charge of heresy which was brought against the Sinai text, even before it was published, has now been all but abandoned by competent scholars. It gave rise to a spirited discussion in the columns of the *Academy* during the winter of 1894–95; and to various ingenious suggestions for reconciling its self-contradictory reading of Matt. i. 16 with its contradictory context. The whole MS. was at first said to be Adoptionist, or Ebionite; but this opinion was formed before scholars had found time to examine the full text. Even the Prince of Darkness is said to be not quite so black as he is painted; and when a hundred scrutinising eyes were focussed, not only on the offending passage, but on the whole MS., the verdict was emphatically reversed by several of the scholars of the day.

I cannot here give a detailed account of the

reasons which have led to this conclusion, but I quote some of the words in which it has been expressed.

Wellhausen says :

"That Sin. (the Sinaitic Codex) in Matt. i. 16 is affected by an Ebionistic tendency, is an untenable supposition, which is contradicted already by the fact, that even in it the story of the birth from the Virgin by the Holy Spirit (who, moreover, is not exactly regarded as father; 'Spirit' in Syriac is a feminine noun, and really signifies 'mother') follows immediately after the genealogy."[1]

Zahn says :

"I am unable to discern any heretical tendencies in Ss. (the Sinai Codex)."[2]

Father Durand says :

"La généalogie qui ouvre l'Évangile selon Saint Matthieu n'est pas une addition postérieure, d'origine ebioniste. . . . Cette altération du texte n'a pas été inspirée par le désir

[1] *Der Syrischc Evangelien-palimpsest vom Sinai*, p. 6, l. 32 (Göttingen, *Nachrichten der K. Gesell. der Wissenschaften*, 1895, Heft 1).

[2] *Theologisches Literaturblatt*, Jan. 16, 1895, p. 29.

de propager l'opinion ebioniste de la génération actuelle du Christ."[1]

A. L. says :

"So apparently we can affirm henceforth, not only the high antiquity, but the perfect orthodoxy of the Sinaitic reading. . . . The significance of the word 'begat' is then a purely legal one. The author of the genealogy could not have employed another word without attenuating the strength of his demonstration."[2]

Dr Rendel Harris himself says, "We should have to reduce the Infancy section to shreds, before it would satisfy an Adoptionist hypothesis.'

The suggestion, first made by Mrs Gibson,[3] that the remarkable reading in Matt. i. 16 may be due to a mistake in translating from a Greek MS., where the word "εγεννησε," meaning either "begat" or "gave birth to," had Mary for its nominative, was afterwards propounded quite independently of her by

[1] *Études Réligieuses*, 15 janvier, 1895, p. 150.

[2] *Bulletin Critique*, 15 juin, 1895, pp. 328, 329.

[3] *Times*, 2nd November.

Dr Zahn. Mr Allen,[1] Dr Rahlfs,[2] Dr Zahn[3] and Dr Skipwith[4] have pointed out that this reading occurs in the Greek cursive MSS. 346–556, and I am glad that Dr Burkitt refers to this as a possible theory in his interesting paper at the Church Congress in October 1895. But I think that the solution which I have propounded is a better one.

With the exception of these verses, Matt. i. 16, 21, and 25, I feel safe in affirming that no charge of heresy can be brought against any part of the Sinai Codex. The expression "my chosen" occurs twice in our English versions (Matt. xii. 18; Luke xxiii. 35), and "my beloved" twice in the Sinai Palimpsest (Mark ix. 7; Luke iii. 18). To be consistent, those who condemn our codex on the strength of Matt. i. 16 ought to put aside all Greek MSS., and all translations which contain the Virgin's words in Luke ii. 48, "*Behold, thy father and I have sought thee sorrowing.*"

[1] *Academy*, 15th December 1894.
[2] *Ibid.*, 29th December 1895, p. 557.
[3] *Theologisches Literaturblatt*, 18th January 1895, vol. 29.
[4] *Academy*, 2nd February 1895, p. 105.

The *Church Quarterly Review* for April 1895 contained a very able and ingenious article on the subject of the Sinai Palimpsest, which was nevertheless written without a full knowledge of all the facts. The reviewer supposed that certain passages had been erased from the manuscript by the monks of a later age, because they were unsound on the question of our Lord's divinity. I am not ungrateful for the kind way in which he has spoken of me personally, but, nevertheless, I am obliged to point out that at the very time he was writing, I was on my way from Sinai to Cambridge, fulfilling his own prophecy, by bringing with me a transcript of some of these very passages on whose supposed obliteration from the manuscript he grounded one of his arguments for its heretical character. Moreover, it did not occur to him that if John the Recluse, or any other orthodox believer, had sat down deliberately to expunge the offending passages in a heretical manuscript, he would surely have begun with Matt. i. 16. Yet the page which contains that verse is one of the clearest and best preserved in the whole palimpsest.

Surely we are not going to shut our eyes, for its sake, to the beautiful picture of our Lord standing while He spoke to the degraded woman of Samaria, nor to the improved chronology of John i. 40–43.

And here I must say, that I, for one, cannot see the cogency of the argument which is sometimes used against the story of the Virgin-birth from the silence about it in the Acts and the Epistles.[1] Paul, Luke, James, and Peter were shrewd, practical men of the world, who were not likely to make a fact, which, by its very nature, was not susceptible of proof, the pivot of their reasoning. Not the Virgin-birth, but the Resurrection, was the mast to which they nailed their colours. Believe that, and all other miracles will seem to you in the highest degree probable ; disprove it, and human life is again overhung by the dark, impenetrable cloud of the shadow of death.

[1] See H. R. Haweis in the *Contemporary Review* for October 1895, p. 600.

CHAPTER IV

VARIANTS IN MATTHEW

In Matt. ii. 2 we have what appears to be a very slight variant, yet it has led to our studying the Greek text more closely. "*For we have seen His star from the east.*" While I was translating this, it suddenly struck me that we can read into the ordinary Greek text, that it was the wise men who were in the east, not the star. Since Dr Adolf Deissmann and Dr James Hope Moulton have discovered, from their examination of the papyrus fragments found by Drs Grenfell and Hunt in the rubbish heaps at Oxyrhynchus, in the Fayoum, Egypt, that the New Testament was written in the language used by the common people of our Lord's day, we may assume that the narrative portion of the Gospels has a looser grammatical construction than the one which we should expect in classical Greek, even if it were of the same period. It is therefore quite possible to translate the statement of the Magi in ver. 2, "*for we, being in the east, have seen His star.*"

We may also read in ver. 9, "*And lo, the star which they had seen, when they were in the east, went before them,*" etc.

How often do we speak in a similar style! Without being quite so narrowly parochial as the Scotch farmer, who became reconciled to living in London when he was walking along the Embankment, and his friend exclaimed, "Losh, man, but that's the Peebles mune!" (moon), we may occasionally assert that we saw Halley's comet at Droitwich. The comet was not specially at Droitwich, but we were there when it became visible to us.

This solves a riddle which has long puzzled me. We do not know where the wise men were when they saw the star, but the title of Magi, given to them in the Greek text, implies either that they belonged to Persia or to Chaldea. If the star had really been to the east of them, would they not have journeyed towards India or China, rather than to Palestine? All heavenly bodies naturally appear to travel from east to west every night; but the wise men would surely have attached no special importance to so common an occurrence. I have formed no opinion as to whether this star was Halley's comet, or an apparent conjunction of stars, or the planet Venus in an imaginary astrological house, or a heavenly body specially created for the purpose. The Syriac text leaves us quite free to speculate on these matters. All that I suggest is, that the star probably appeared in the western heavens, and that in consequence the wise men journeyed towards Palestine.

In this reading of the Greek text I am fortified by the opinion of Dr Deissmann, who was on a visit to us at the time when this idea occurred to me; and who said, "You are quite right, the Greek text can be read in that way."

If the wise men started from Chaldæa, they would spend about three months in crossing the desert before they approached the frontier of

Southern Palestine. How did they lose sight of the star? Some people think that the rain-clouds, which frequently cover the Syrian sky in spring, hid it from their view. But I imagine they were so possessed with the idea that the king of the Jews must be born in Herod's palace, that they ceased for some days to follow its guidance.

And here I must observe that in speaking of the Syrian sky, I have myself given an example of the familiar, but incorrect, way of writing which I suppose the Evangelist Matthew to have used in vers. 2 and 8. I am not worse, however, than Matthew Arnold, the great critic, who says of our Lord:

> "Now He is dead. Far hence He lies,
> By a lorn Syrian town;
> And on His grave, with shining eyes,
> The Syrian stars look down."

Till the time of the travellers' departure from Jerusalem, we need not suppose that the star had even appeared to move, except for its nightly progress westwards. Suppose, however, that it was south-east of Jerusalem when the

Magi again recognised it. They would not have more than seven miles to go before reaching Beth Leḥem, whose name they had just learned from the chief priests and scribes of the nation; men who had neither sufficient curiosity, nor sufficient faith in the prophecy of Micah to accompany them. Zahn points out (*Ev. des Matthäus*, p. 99) that the star is not said to have stood over any particular house, but "*over where the young child was.*" "Where" may mean the village.

Having arrived at its gate, they would ask the few men who had occasion to return to their homes about sunset, or more probably some women who were fetching water for their households, if there was in any house a boy exactly three months and so many days old, according to the time when they had first seen the star, and they would then be directed, not to the inn, nor to the cave near it which was used as a stable, but to some more comfortable dwelling to which the Holy Family had migrated. We are not told by what signs they recognised the Babe.

They had doubtless some spiritual admonition, and it was probably strengthened by the questions which they put to Joseph and Mary about the Child's ancestry.

I would add, that if you try to walk in the direction of a star, it will always appear to recede from you.

In Matt. iv. 23, 24 we read, "*And Jesus went round about in all Galilee, teaching in their synagogues, and preaching the Gospel of the kingdom, and healing all disease and all sickness which were among the people. And they brought near unto Him many that were tormented with hateful torments, and with sore sicknesses; and on each of them He laid His hand; and He healed every one.*"

Our Lord's miracles were not done in wholesale fashion. Each case was treated separately. We never read of anyone being cured who did not come into personal contact with Him, either directly or through a friend.

"And the report of Him went forth into all Syria" is here omitted.

In Matt. v. 22, "*without a cause*" of the Authorised Version is also in the Sinai text.

This is supported by a famous group of Greek cursive MSS., by Codex Bezæ, and Codex L; also by all the Old Latin MSS. We cannot help wishing that our Revisers had retained it; for however well we may be enabled by grace to curb our anger, it would be a superhuman virtue to feel none when we are really wronged.

Ver. 5 of chap. vi. is omitted from this text. It may be merely a repetition of ver. 3.

The meaning of Matt. vi. 7, "*And when ye pray, do not say vain things, like the heathen: who think that with much speaking they shall be heard,*" is nearly the same as in our English Revised Version. Yet the two Syriac words used to represent the one Greek word βαττολογήσητε, "say vain things," have enabled Dr Blass, of Halle, to suggest better derivations for that word than any which we find in a Greek lexicon, and thereby to determine its exact significance. It does not come from βάττος, "a stammerer." Our Lord surely did not tell His disciples not to stammer in prayer; for the word is one of those hybrid compounds which come into existence in countries where two or more languages are in common use. It is formed by the Aramaic word "b'tal," "vain, useless," and by the Greek verb λογέω, from λόγος, "a word." The word "b'tal" is from a Semitic root, which appears also in Hebrew and in Arabic. Few words are more frequently on the lips of the modern Syrians and Egyptians; whether it be used of the refuse which is thrown into the gutters, or of a neighbour who has incurred the speaker's dislike. "Nâs b'tal" is almost equivalent to "canaille." I once had the pleasure of hearing myself called "es-sitt el-b'talat." It was during our return journey from Mount Sinai in 1902, when I had cut my right hand badly in breaking a glass bottle, and could not spring up on my camel as heretofore, while holding the horn of the saddle. I had to be lifted; so by way of distinction, the Bedawîn spoke of me as "es-sitt el-b'talat," while my more nimble sister was "es-sitt es-saghirat." It is not against repetition that we are warned in this verse, but against a clatter of the lips which the heart does not accompany.

In chap. viii. vers. 5, 8, 13, the centurion, or captain of a hundred, is called a *chiliarch*, or captain of a thousand.

In Matt. viii. 24 we read, "*And there was a great tempest in the lake and it* (the ship) *was almost covered with the waves.*" The use of the word "lake," instead of "sea" is a peculiarity of the Sinai Palimpsest, not shared by any other MS.

In Matt. viii. 29 we are told that the demons "*cried with a loud voice, saying, What have we to do with Thee, Thou Son of God? Art Thou come hither to make us ashamed?*"

In Matt. ix. 11 we learn that the Pharisees asked our Lord's disciples, "*Wherefore with publicans and sinners are ye eating and drinking?*"

In chap. xvi. the greater part of ver. 2 and the whole of ver. 3 are omitted, as they are also in the two oldest of the Greek uncials and in an important group of Greek cursives.

I regret greatly that before the Sinai MS. was turned into a palimpsest, *i.e.* before A.D. 778, it unfortunately lost the leaf which must have contained Matt. xvi. 18. But we are happily not without a witness as to what the reading of the Old Syriac here was. The Curetonian MS., which is supposed to give us a revision of the Sinai text, and the Peshiṭta, which is the Authorised Version of the Syriac Church, agree about it word for word.

We must explain that the Syriac language has two genders only, the masculine and the feminine; the feminine doing duty for the neuter. It is well known that Kepha, "a stone" (rather than "a rock"), is feminine. But St Peter can never in Syriac be mistaken for a stone; because, where he is furnished with a verb or with a relative pronoun, these are always in the masculine; whereas, when a stone is meant, these adjuncts are feminine,—just as in French we say, "cette pierre a été roulée," but in the case of a boy, "Ce Pierre est méchant." Apply this simple rule to the text of Matthew's Gospel, and what result do you get?

We cannot use this touchstone in English, for our language has none of these grammatical niceties. The feminine, as I have said, does duty for the neuter; and in the case of a phrase being nominative to a verb, that verb, and any relative pronoun which represents the phrase, would be feminine.

Let us, then, try to put Matt. xvi. 19 into literal French—a language with which many of my readers must be acquainted. "Et moi je te dis aussi, que tu es le Pierre, et sur cette pierre je bâtirai mon Église."

It is evident that Peter's confession, not Peter himself, is grammatically represented by "cette pierre," and that the Syriac Versions simply and strongly support the view of this passage held by the ancient Orthodox Church of the East, and also by the Reformed Churches of the West.

In chap. xviii. ver. 17, we have, "*Tell it unto the synagogue; and if he* (*i.e.* the sinning brother) *will not hear the synagogue, let him be accounted by thee as a heathen and as a publican.*"

Here the word used is "k'nushta," the plural of which is translated "synagogues" in Matt. vi. 5, whilst its singular stands for "synagogue" in twenty-two other passages of the other three Gospels. We find an altogether different word used for "church" where "church" is meant; and that word occurs in this verse, both in the Curetonian and in the Peshiṭta. These, however, are later than the Sinai text; and have been subjected to revision for the purpose of bringing them into harmony with the Greek MSS. Synagogues existed in our Lord's day; they had sprung up during the Babylonian captivity, and had become a feature of Jewish national life. How natural it was that He should have counselled an appeal to one of them, rather than to a "church" which was not then constituted! And was it not equally natural that in later times, when the Church had taken the place of the synagogue, the new title should have been read into this passage? Yet to us its occurrence here is a real anachronism.

The text of Matt. xviii. 20 occurs on a spot where the vellum has been much damaged; so that there has been some difference of opinion concerning it among the transcribers. But there is now little doubt that it reads, with Codex Bezæ, "*For there are not two or three gathered together in My name, and I am not amongst them.*"

In Matt. xix. 4 we find, "*Have ye not read, that He who made the male, made also the female?*"

In Matt. xx. 15 we have, "*Have I not power to do what I will in My house?*" instead of "with Mine own?" This was the reading of Tatian's Diatessaron, as we know from Ephraim's Commentary on it.

In Matt. xx. 16 the Sinai text agrees with the Authorised Version in retaining "*Many be called, but few chosen.*"

In Matt. xx. 33 we have the story of the two importunate blind men, who were healed by our Lord. The Sinai Palimpsest has lost the leaf which ought to contain this passage. We cannot therefore tell if it confirms the beautiful variant of Cureton's MS., "*They say unto Him, Our Lord, that our eyes may be opened, and we may see Thee.*"

In Matt. xxi. 31, after the parable of the two

sons who were told to go and work in their father's vineyard, our Lord asked, "*Whether of these did the will of his father? They say unto Him, The last.*" This strange reply is the reading of Codex Vaticanus, Codex Bezæ, the Ferrar group of Greek cursives, and most of the Old Latin MSS. The Ferrar MSS. show us how it came about. By some misadventure, in a very early MS., a copyist placed the story of the willing, but disobedient son before that of the unwilling but obedient one. Then a copyist of his work, seeing the mistake, put it right, but forgot to transpose the answers. Dr Nestle evidently thinks that the Ferrar group gives us the true arrangement; for he has incorporated it in the British and Foreign Bible Society's Greek text of the New Testament which he has edited. I give it for the sake of those who have not access to the original. "But how does it seem to you? A certain man had two sons. And he came to the first, and said, Son, go to-day and work in the vineyard. But he answered and said, I will, sir, and went not. And he came to the second, and said likewise. And he answered and said, I will not, (and) afterwards repented and went. Which of the twain did the will of the father? They said, The last."

How such a transposition has come about is not easy to see. I have a suspicion that the Ἐγώ, Κύριε, which represents the answer of the willing but disobedient son in ver. 29 of Nestle's text, may be a corruption of Ὑπάγω, Κύριε, the first syllable of Ὑπάγω having been indicated by a contraction, which some copyist misunderstood and omitted.

In Matt. xxi. 32 we have a curious rendering of our Lord's words to the chief priests and elders: "*And ye, when ye saw it* (*i.e.* the publicans and harlots believing in John), *ye at last repented yourselves, that ye might believe in him.*"

Quite possibly they were proud and stiff-necked people, who became convinced about the truth of John's mission because of the crowd who went after him; or because of the changed lives which they observed as a result of his preaching.

In Matt. xxiii. 13 we have a reading which seems to me as if it might be the original one. "*But woe unto you, scribes and Pharisees, hypocrites! for ye hold the key of the kingdom of heaven before men; for ye neither enter in, nor those that are coming do ye suffer them to enter.*"

This is no inapt description of the official position and of the conduct of not a few worldly-minded priests in the Christian Church before the Reformation. The state of the Jewish nation, in our Lord's time, from a spiritual point of view, must have been deplorable. It has been well said, that "its priests were Sadducees, and its teachers Pharisees."

In Matt. xxv. 1 we are told that the ten virgins "*went forth to meet the bridegroom and the bride.*" This is the reading of the Peshiṭta, Codex Bezæ, an important group of Greek cursives, the Vulgate, and most of the Old Latin MSS. It is not of great importance, because the wedding procession was from the house of the bridegroom to that of the bride's father, and thence back to the bridegroom's house; so that each of the ten virgins may have intended to join it in an informal manner at the point where it passed nearest to her dwelling; and all of them might well do so during the latter part of its course, when both of the leading figures in the ceremony were present.

In Matt. xxvi. 10 our Lord says of the woman who had poured sweet ointment on His head, "*She hath wrought a beautiful, a good work on Me.*"

Matt. xxvi. 28, "*This is My blood, the new testament.*" This agrees with the text of St Luke and St Paul, who both say, "*This is the new testament in My blood.*" In the Sinai text, therefore, that curious expression, "*This is My blood, of the new testament,*" occurs only in the Gospel of St Mark.

Matt. xxvi. 71, instead of "And when he (*i.e.* Peter) was gone out into the porch," we have "*And when he had gone out to the door of the court.*"

Matt. xxvii. 9.—In this verse the Sinai text certainly shows that the Evangelist Matthew did not make a mistake which is often too readily attributed to him. Its reading is, "*Then was fulfilled that which was spoken by the prophet, who said, I took the thirty pieces of silver, the price of him who was valued, which I was valued at by the children of Israel; and I gave them for the field of the potter, as the Lord commanded me.*"

There is no mention here of Jeremiah. It is thus evident that the copyist of an early Greek text had Matt. ii. 17 in his mind when he came to this passage; and repeated "*by Jeremy the prophet*," having already written it about the weeping Rachel.

"Jeremiah" in Matt. xxvii. 9 is omitted also by the Peshiṭta, the Diatessaron, and by the two earliest of the Old Latin MSS.; also by one of two Lessons in a Greek Lectionary MS. in Christ's College, Cambridge.

It seems to me that we ought always to give to an author the benefit of a doubt, and especially to one who has helped to give us the divinely inspired oracles. Pens slip very readily when they are held in human hands; and when we find a large class of Biblical manuscripts which are free from a patent mistake, we ought to judge that the said mistake is a corruption of the original; and refrain from citing it as a witness against the inspiration of the New Testament.

The same remark will apply to the parallel case of Mark i. 2. Perhaps the MSS. which lie behind our English Authorised Version are only four in number; but they are by no means singular in saying, "*As it is written in the prophets*," without attributing the words of Malachi to Isaiah. Unfortunately we cannot now tell if the mistake was present in the Old Syriac Version, for the beginning of St Mark's Gospel was on a page which has been lost from the Sinai Palimpsest; and the whole of this Gospel is missing from the Curetonian MS., with the exception of the last four verses, Mark xvi. 17–20, which very probably do not belong to St Mark at all.

In Matt. xxvii. 16, 17 we have the name of the robber whom the countrymen of our Lord preferred to Himself, as *Jesus Bar-abba*. Here certainly a fact has been preserved. It is confirmed by the Palestinian Syriac Version, and by a passage in Bar Bahlul (Duval, col. 423). There we are told that it is so written in the *Gospel of the separated.* But how did a robber get the name of "Jesus"? Perhaps it was because of his daring character, which had led the Jews to hope that he might become their saviour from the Romans.

In Matt. xxvii. 56 we find among the names of the women who followed our Lord from Galilee, ministering unto Him, "*Mary Magdalene, and Mary the daughter of James and the mother of Joseph, and the mother of the children of Zebedee.*"

The second of these Maries is called "Mary the *daughter* of James" elsewhere in this manuscript: in Mark xv. 40, xvi. 1. The same phenomenon is found in the Palestinian Syriac Version in all these places. We believe that this text gives us the correct rendering of the Greek Μαρία ἡ τοῦ Ἰακώβου. Although nothing is more common in Semitic nations than for a man to be known as the father of his first-born son, or a woman as the child's mother, many of them, in fact, changing their names on the birth of their offspring, the meaning of the Greek phrase, "she of James," certainly is that she was either the daughter or the wife of a man who bore the name of his ancestral patriarch. A woman in modern Greece follows the ancient custom of never being in the nominative case as regards her surname; she is always the chattel either of her father or of her husband, and is therefore perpetually in the genitive. But she stands in no such relation to any of her children. A man's name is in the genitive case until his father's death. Thereafter he can lift up his head, and be a nominative. For these reasons, I submit that to call Mary the mother of James is a transgression of Greek grammar and of the dictates of Greek custom.

CHAPTER V

VARIANTS IN MARK

THE Sinai text has fewer remarkable variants in the Gospel of Mark than it has in the other three. Yet there are some things which are worthy of attention.

In Mark ii. 26, "*in the days when Abiathar was high priest*" is omitted, and this removes an alleged difficulty. We have no sure ground for believing that Abiathar was high priest when he permitted David to eat the shew-bread.

In Mark iv. 5, 6 we read of the seed which fell on the rock, "*And because there was no depth of earth below its root, and it sprouted in the sun that was on it, and it withered.*"

In chap. vii. ver. 26, we are told that the Syro-Phœnician woman, whose daughter was healed by our Lord in response to the mother's importunity, was a widow. We might have guessed this, from the circumstance that no mention is made of her husband ; and while it is true that the omission of one letter in "widow" would give us the word for "heathen," it is equally true that the word for "widow" is quite distinct.

In Mark viii. 31, 32 Dr Burkitt has drawn attention to a remarkable variant, "*And they will kill Him, and the third day He will rise and openly speak the word.*" It is supported by a similar reading in the Arabic Version of the Diatessaron ; and Codex Bobbiensis (k) has "et a scribis et occidit, post tertium diem resurgere, et cum fiducia sermonem loqui." This would imply a prophecy that our Lord would Himself preach publicly after His resurrection, a prophecy which He has fulfilled only through the agency of His disciples. With all my partiality for the Sinai Palimpsest, I feel that in this particular case the reading of the Greek MSS., "*And He spake the saying openly*," is much better. The imperfect tense of the verb ἐλάλει, which they use, signifies that our Lord spoke publicly of His impending crucifixion and resurrection not once, but several times; and it is very satisfactory for us to know that the Evangelist Mark was able to record this as an unchallenged fact. The variant might easily arise from a mistake on the part of some Syrian or Latin translator, who, finding no punctuation, no accents, no separation of words in a Greek uncial manuscript, divided the sentence wrongly, and, wishing to make sense, added one letter, or even two, to ἐλάλει, so as to make it into the infinitive ἐκλαλεῖν, which Dr Burkitt has suggested as being the original form.

In Mark ix. 39, when John made a complaint about a man who was casting out demons in our Lord's name, and yet did not follow His disciples, Jesus replied, "*Forbid him not, for there is no man who doeth anything in My name, and is able to speak evil against Me.*" It is great encouragement for ordinary Christians to know that anything done in our Lord's name will receive His recognition. It need not be a mighty work; it may be only the giving of a cup of cold water.

It is also possible to follow Jesus without following His disciples. I have heard a suggestion, probably from the Rev. G. A. Johnstone Ross, that this man may have been cheated by Judas, or may have received a snub either from the impetuous Peter, or from one of the ambitious sons of Zebedee. The aspiring family of that master fisherman is recalled to us by a variant in chap. x. ver. 40, in our Lord's reply to their mother, Salome, "*But to sit on My right hand or on My left, this is not mine to give, but for another it is prepared.*" The word translated "another" is masculine singular.

In chap. x. vers. 46-52, we have the story of "Timai Bar Timai," the blind beggar, who, when the bystanders said unto him, "Fear not, rise, He calleth thee," "*rose, took up his garment, and came to Jesus.*" He did not cast away his "*abbaya*," or sheepskin mantle; no, he put it on. When the Sinai text was first published, we were confidently told that this had sprung from the imperfect knowledge of the Greek language possessed by the Syrian translator, who had mistaken the word ἀπολαβὼν for ἀποβαλὼν. I felt sure that it was no such thing; for I have watched too closely the habits of Orientals not to know that they will more readily put on some outer garment when they are summoned into the presence of a superior than divest themselves of anything. I have sometimes tried to photograph a picturesque group of Bedawîn squatting on the sand, in the days before either my sister or I possessed a snap-shotting Kodak. These men would be quite at their ease so long as the lens of our camera was directed to the mountain, Râs-es-Sufsafeh. But when we had asked permission to take their own portraits, and were shifting our camera, with its tripod, so as to turn its eye on them, they occupied themselves with an effort to look respectable; put on their goats-hair *abbayas*, and spread the edges of these quite decently over a miscellaneous lot of bare legs and arms. And behold! by the time we were ready to remove the cap from our lens, we had got before us a prosaic group of very common-looking people. I was therefore much pleased when Dr Burkitt announced that he had found the word ἐπιλαβὼν in a cursive Greek MS. used of Bar-Timai's action in this very verse. I was then told by an Irish friend that this variant would have awful consequences. "Do you not know," he said, "that the new reading of Mark x. 50 threatens to destroy whole cart-loads of books on divinity?" "Why so?" I asked. "Because the old divines used to say that we must cast away our own righteousness before we can come to the Saviour; and our own righteousness is represented by the cloak of Bar-Timæus." "Well, I am not sorry," I replied. "There are plenty of texts in the Bible which teach us that truth, especially in St Paul's Epistles. You do not need to distort the story of a real occurrence for the purpose of enforcing it. Bar-Timai knew nothing about such teaching at the time he either took off or put on his cloak. And all who have watched Eastern ways will say, that it is much more likely that he put it on. The great point is that he rose, and came to Jesus. By allegorising a story too much, we sometimes weaken our own conviction that we are dealing with real history."

In Mark xii. 38 we read, "*Keep yourselves from the scribes, who love to walk in the porches* (stoæ), *and love greetings in the market-places,*" etc. Here the difference is between stoæ, "porches," and stolæ, "long robes." We cannot tell which word our Lord used. There was at least one porch in Jerusalem called by the name of Solomon; it was on the edge of the artificially flattened top of Mount Moriah, within the Temple area, and it appears to have been a favourite resort of our Lord, and also of His disciples after His Ascension. Possibly the right word has been preserved in the Syriac text.

In Mark xiii. 9 our Lord says, "*And they shall deliver you up to the people, and to councils; and ye shall stand before kings, and ye shall be beaten before governors for My sake.*" The word "people" is found in no other extant text, but after reading the story of St Paul's sufferings at the hands of his own countrymen in Jerusalem (Acts xxi. 32), and in more than one city of Asia Minor, no one can say for certain that it has been wrongly attributed to our Lord, or that it is in any sense an interpolation.

In Mark xiv. 41 we read about the agony in the garden of Gethsemane, "*And he cometh the third time, and saith unto them, Sleep, and take your rest: the hour is come; the end is at hand; behold! the Son of man is betrayed into the hands of sinners.*"

This variant, "*the end is at hand,*" is shared by a few Old Latin MSS., and by the Peshiṭta, which, since the beginning of the fifth century, has been the Authorised Version of the Syrian Church. It has been called the "Queen of the Versions," and it is certainly pre-eminent in one particular: it has scarcely a variant, except in the matter of spelling. A copy of the Peshiṭta written by one of Bishop Rabbula's scribes in the fifth century A.D., is the same as the last edition published in England, whether of the Gospels, by Mr Gwilliam, or of the whole New Testament, by C. Schaaf.

Those who cling to the verbal infallibility of the divine oracles might indeed comfort themselves by getting a copy of Murdock's translation of the Peshiṭta Version into English. But I may as well tell them that this absolute faithfulness to the letter of the law has produced no burning zeal for its promulgation among the heathen ; and it has not preserved the Church which owns the Peshiṭta either from the so-called Monophysite heresy, or from degrading superstition. For instance, a case has been known of a Bishop who was too ill to travel to a distant city where some candidates for the priesthood were waiting for ordination. The difficulty was overcome by getting the sick Bishop to breathe into the mouth of a bottle. The bottle was then tightly corked, and carried to the church where the priests were in waiting. Who performed the ordination ceremony, rumour saith not, but the Bishop's part was held to be duly fulfilled when the uncorked bottle was held over the heads of the neophytes. This ignorant folly must not, however, blind us to the fact that the Syrian Church of the East has been far more faithful to her trust in the transmission of the Bible text than the Latin-speaking Church of the West. The

Vulgate has suffered more than one revision to bring it into harmony with its own earliest MSS. The Peshiṭta has never needed revision; though it is supposed to be itself a revision of the Old Syriac—the very text with which we are now dealing. For, in truth, the Syrians, under the guidance of Bishop Rabbula, and others before him, sought to obliterate the evidence of their own ancient version by assimilating it, as far as they could, to the Greek MSS. which were extant in their day, and possibly none of these were much older than the Greek MSS. which we now possess.

In Mark xiv. 56–58 we have, "*Many bare false witness against Him, and their witness agreed not together; but people rose up against Him, saying, We heard Him say, I will destroy the temple that is made with hands,*" etc. We observe that the second "*bare false witness*" is omitted. I think rightly, for those who repeated what our Lord had said about destroying the temple, though they spoke maliciously, were perhaps not bearing false witness. Possibly some over-zealous scribe, in copying one of the oldest of Greek MSS., repeated the "bare false witness" (ἐψευδομαρτύρουν) of ver. 56 also in ver. 57.

Mark xv. 3.—"*And the chief priests accused Him of many things: but He gave them no answer.*" The last clause of this verse resembles a reading of our Authorised Version, which the Revisers have suppressed. It is found in the Ferrar group of Greek cursives, and in the Old Latin a and c.

Mark xv. 39.—"*Now when the centurion, who was standing beside Him, saw Him crying out and expiring, he said, Truly this was the Son of God.*" The "crying out" is in agreement with the Authorised Version, as against the Revised one; with A, C, D, and with some of the best Greek cursives and Old Latin MSS.

In Mark xv. 40, 47, xvi. 1, as in Matt. xxvii. 56, we have, "*Mary the daughter of James the Less.*"

In Mark xv. 42, 43, instead of "And when even was now come (because it was the Preparation, that is, the day before the Sabbath), Joseph of Arimathea," etc., we have, "*And it was on the sabbath. And Joseph came from Ramatha,"* etc. This doubtless means that our Lord's burial took place after sunset on the Friday night. I cannot attempt to explain this. But if His body was laid in the grave when the sun was just disappearing (a very appropriate time), so as to leave it a matter of doubt when the Sabbath actually began, the discrepancy between this reading and that of Luke xxiii. 54, "*And that day was the Preparation, and the sabbath was dawning,*"[1] would be accounted for. So would also the delay of the women to perform those last offices of love which we read about in Mark xvi. 1. Is it possible that the Sinai Codex gives the true reading of Mark's narrative, and that the form found in Greek MSS. is an attempt to harmonise it with that of Luke?

In Mark xvi. 3 we read that the women said among themselves, "*But who shall roll us away the stone of the sepulchre? for it was very great.*" The last clause of this verse seems to be here in its true and original place, *i.e.* in the thoughts of the women, whence it wandered,

[1] Or "*drew on.*"

at a very early period, to the end of ver. 4. Possibly a scribe left it out by accident, and afterwards inserted it on the margin; then a later scribe, copying his work, embodied it in the text at the wrong place. Codex Bezæ, and the Palestinian Syriac Version have it also at the end of ver. 3; whilst the Gospel of Pseudo-Peter, published in 1892, actually puts it into the speech of the women as they walked to the sepulchre, instead of only into their thoughts, as it is here.

In Mark xvi. 8, "And fled from the tomb; for trembling and astonishment had come upon them" is omitted.

In Mark xvi. 8 we read, "*And when they had heard, they went out; and went, and said nothing to any man; for they were afraid.*"

"*Here endeth the Gospel of Mark.*" And after a row of red stops, we have on the same narrow column, also in red, "*The Gospel of Luke.*"

The omission of vers. 9–20 is the more surprising, because vers. 17–20 are the only portion of St Mark's Gospel which is extant in the Curetonian manuscript. On this subject, which has given rise to so much discussion among scholars, it may be presumptuous in me to venture an opinion ; but, apart from the fact that a name, that of Ariston the Presbyter, has been found by Mr F. C. Conybeare attached to this section, in an Armenian MS. of Etchmiadzin, I think that they put into the mouth of our Lord some words which it would be difficult for anyone to justify : for the promise contained in vers. 17, 18 has not been fulfilled. It is indeed recorded that the signs here described did follow the Apostles and early disciples ; but, after the first century, we have no trustworthy historical evidence that they followed anyone who believed. Why did miracles of healing cease with the Apostolic age ? I have a theory on the subject which is at least not more fanciful than some which I have met with. It is this :—

Jesus Christ, being the Son of God, was, even in His human body, the source of all the life in the universe—animal life as well as moral and spiritual. An inexhaustible, vital power lay hidden under His humble exterior. He could exert or repress it at will; but repression was not the usual impulse of His loving heart. Sinners felt uncomfortable in His presence; they shrank from His direct gaze; and bodily disease, which springs from decay and corruption, was simply arrested by this ever-flowing stream of vital force which, emanating from His person, flowed into the persons of those who came near Him. Bodily defects were thrown off by the people who were thus quickened. And something of this force remained with those who had been much in His society, gradually subsiding as the years rolled on. Thus the power of healing the sick by the laying on of hands was possessed by the Apostles, but it could not be transmitted to those who had not seen God manifest in the flesh.

In Cureton's manuscript the Gospel of John follows that of Mark, and is in its turn followed by that of Luke. The Sinai Palimpsest, on the contrary, shows us the four Gospels in the order familiar to us. Why do these two representatives of the Old Syriac Version differ from each other on so important a point? They are linked and yet separate. Their relation to each other, and to the Diatessaron, and to the Peshiṭta, will for some time continue to present a fruitful field for discussion.

CHAPTER VI

VARIANTS IN LUKE

Of only one ancient manuscript can it be said that it is perfect, and has never lost a leaf. That one, strange to say, is the Codex Sinaiticus, the Greek manuscript of the whole Bible, *plus* the Epistle of Barnabas, and part of the Shepherd of Hermas, which was found by Constantine Tischendorf in the very same monastery of St Catherine, on Mount Sinai, where, half a century later, I found the Old Syriac text of the Gospels. This fact, to my mind, shows that there was some exaggeration in Tischendorf's tale about its being in a waste-paper basket. A basket, if you please! but not one intended to contain rubbish! I became aware —and possibly my habit of constantly talking modern Greek with my twin-sister, Mrs

Gibson, made the monks more communicative to us than their predecessors were to Tischendorf—that these holy fathers had a habit of keeping nearly all their manuscripts in boxes ; a practice which made it difficult for them to find one on short notice ; and that those MSS. which had lost their bindings were consigned to baskets ; but not with the least intention of throwing them away. As for the famous document being in an outhouse, there is now scarcely a room in the whole monastery which does not deserve that description ; for almost every apartment within the quadrangle of its walls has a door opening to the outer air.

Unlike the Greek Sinaiticus, this Syriac MS. had the misfortune to lose seventeen of its leaves, in the days before a second Syriac text was written over the Gospel one, and it was turned into a palimpsest, or twice-scraped thing. Note that the vellum was polished with pumice-stone, once in the fourth century, to prepare its surface for receiving the text of the Gospels ; then again in the seventh or eighth century, to cover that Gospel up and hide it under the

Tales of Holy Women. It may have been for this very reason, viz. that because of careless treatment, seventeen of its leaves had dropped away, John the Stylite considered it chiefly fit for being used as writing material.

On the very last page, at the end of a line, we find the date of the later writing. At the spot where this occurs there is a hole in the vellum, and this makes it impossible for us to tell whether the date is 1009 or 1090 after Alexander the Great. If a flourish occurred in the script at the end of this line, such as may be seen on many other pages of the book, the date would undoubtedly be 1009, as I read it when left entirely to my own devices in 1892; but if the syllable "în" stood where the hole now is, as Dr Rendel Harris supposes, we must acquiesce in its being 1090, *i.e.* in the eighth century. From that time no one can possibly have read a syllable of the fourth-century Gospel text beneath it, until I detected our Lord's name, viz. "*Jesus the Messiah*," in 1892, and proceeded further to decipher the words, "*Verily, verily, I say unto you*," words which made me sure that the dirty pages which I had been exploring contained an early text of the Gospels.

In the first chapter of St Luke's Gospel vers. 16–38 are on one of the lost leaves.

The Magnificat, spoken by Mary, runs thus (vers. 46–55): "*My soul doth magnify the Lord, and my spirit hath rejoiced in God the Saviour. Who hath regarded the lowliness of His handmaiden. For from henceforth all generations shall call me blessed. For He hath done to me great things; He who by name is glorious and holy, whose mercy is unto the generation and on the tribe to those who fear Him. And He hath shewed strength with His arm: and hath scattered the imagination of the hearts of the proud ones. He hath put down the mighty from their seats, and hath exalted the humble. And He hath filled the poor with His good things; and the rich He hath despised when in want. And He hath cared for His son Israel, and hath remembered His mercy: as He spake to our fathers, to Abraham, and to his seed for ever.*"

In ver. 63, "*And they all marvelled*" is

transferred from the end of ver. 63 to the end of ver. 64. It is thus described as the effect of Zacharias' tongue being loosed, rather than of his writing that his son's name was John. The phrase has perhaps suffered a transposition similar to that about the size of the stone in Mark xvi. 3, 4. In two old Latin MSS., the Vercellensis and Veronensis, this phrase comes after the word "*loosened*" and before "*And his mouth was opened.*" This last phrase does not occur in the Sinai text.

Thus we have at the end of ver. 64, "*And straightway the string of his tongue was loosened, and he blessed God, and they all marvelled.*"

In Luke i. 80, it is said of John the Baptist, "*And he fled into the desert until the day of his shewing unto Israel.*"

In chap. ii. ver. 4 we read, "*And Joseph also went up from Nazareth, a city of Galilee, to Judæa, to the city of David, which is called Beth Leḥem, he and Mary his wife, being great with child, that there they might be enrolled, because they were both of the house of David.*" Here the word used for "wife" is more explicit than either the ἐμνηστευμένῃ of the Greek MSS. or the "espoused" of the Peshiṭta. It shows clearly that Mary was under the full legal protection of Joseph.

In Luke ii. 8 we read how "*shepherds were there in that place, and they were awake, and were keeping watch over their ewes.*"

In ver. 12 the angel says to them, "*Behold, I give you a sign.*"

In Luke ii. 14 we have, "*Ana goodwill to men,*" the reading of our Authorised Version; εὐδοκία, instead of εὐδοκίας (with Codex Vaticanus, Codex L, and some important cursive Greek MSS. (*fam.* 1), the Peshiṭta, the Palestinian Syriac, and the Coptic).

It seems to me that both readings, "*goodwill to men,*" and "*to men of goodwill,*" have in them an eternal truth. God, who willeth not the death of a sinner, proclaimed His "*goodwill to men*" by the human birth of our Lord. At the same time, it is only "*men of goodwill*" who accept His wonderful gift, and therefore it is they only who enjoy peace.

In ver. 15 we are told that the shepherds

said one to another, "*Come, let us go to Beth Leḥem and see this thing which is come to pass as the angel hath shewed us.*"

I submit that these words are more suitable than "*as the Lord hath made known unto us.*" We are not told that they had heard the voice of God in any way. Is it not more natural that they should speak of the angel whose song of praise was still ringing in their ears?

In ver. 35 we have a very curious reading, which, so far as we know, does not occur anywhere else. It is in the blessing pronounced on Mary by Simeon: "*And through thine own soul thou shalt cause a spear to pass.*"

This may possibly be the original form of the passage. Those Christians who pay an undue adoration to the Virgin Mary, who, in fact, call her "Mother of God," cannot be expected to see that some time before the Crucifixion took place, she was partly the authoress of her own woes. For, like many another fond mother, she tried to control and restrain Him after He had taken the thread of His destiny into His own hands; and one cannot help thinking that if she had understood Him better, if, in short, she had maintained the sublime faith which she exhibited at the time of the Annunciation and during her subsequent trials, she would have saved both herself and Him from some needless pain. I do not, of course, refer to her sufferings at the time of His Crucifixion, but only to the incident related in Matt. xii. 46–50. The word "spear" occurs also in the Peshiṭta; the Curetonian MS. being here deficient. But the idea of Mary being an active agent in the piercing of her own heart is peculiar to the Sinai Codex, and could not have been imagined at a period later than the second century. How natural it is that the repeated revisions of the Old Syriac should have improved it away!

In chap. ii. ver. 36, we have another unique reading. It is said of Anna the prophetess, "*And seven days only was she with a husband after her virginity; and the rest of her life was she in widowhood, eighty and four years.*"

Startling as this variant is, it may yet be the true reading. A marriage which lasts only seven years is no uncommon thing, and if the same portion of wedded happiness had been allotted to Anna as to thousands of other women, this fact would have hardly been worth recording in a narrative so concise as Luke's is. But the mention of *seven days* shows us that Anna's experience had been by no means a common one.

In vers. 41, 42 we have, "*And His parents* (or kinsfolk) *went every year to Jerusalem at the feast of unleavened bread of the passover. And when He was twelve years old, they went up, as was their wont, to the feast. And when they had fulfilled the days of the feast, they returned, and the boy Jesus tarried behind them in Jerusalem; and His parents knew it not.*"

The Syriac word translated "parents" may possibly mean "kinsfolk." (It is found also in the Palestinian Syriac, the Peshiṭta having "and Joseph and his mother.")

In chap. iii. vers. 4–6, the quotation from Isa. xl. 3–5 runs thus: "*Make ye ready a way for the Lord, and make straight in the plain a path for our God*" (with the Curetonian and the

Peshiṭta). "*All the valleys shall be filled, the mountains and the hills shall be brought low; the rough shall become smooth, and the difficult places plains; and the glory of the Lord shall be revealed, and all flesh shall see it together*" (almost with the Curetonian, but without its addition of "because the mouth of the Lord hath spoken," both being nearer to Isa. xl. 4, 5 than other manuscripts are. This is a very good instance for those who judge the Curetonian text to be an amplification of the Sinai one).

In Luke iii. ver. 9, we read, "*And behold, the axe hath reached unto the root of the trees*" (with the Curetonian).

And in ver. 14, "*Do violence to no man, and do injury to no man; let your wages suffice for you*" (with the Curetonian).

This seems to me a better rendering than "be content with your wages." Soldiers are not forbidden to ask higher wages from the Government; but they are exhorted not to supplement their wages by living at the expense of the people on whom they are quartered. I know from personal observation that this habit prevails in the Sultan's army. Several years ago, in 1896, Mrs Gibson and I rode from Egypt to Palestine over what is called by dragomans "the short desert." Stones were thrown at us by some Moslem youths while we were passing through a cemetery on the outskirts of the town of Gaza. The whirligigs, swings, and merry-go-rounds common to an English fair were jingling among the tombstones; so that we could not be accused of being the first to disturb the quiet of a graveyard. Nevertheless, the crowd looked so angry that we thought it prudent to apply to the Governor for a guard of two soldiers to watch over our tents, which were pitched in a field close by. We retained one of these men to ride with us for four days as far as Bittir, on the Jaffa-Jerusalem railway. He explained to us that he had to provide his own horse, but the peasant families on whom he was quartered for the night had to feed both it and him. He would just say "Bring me a chicken," and when he had eaten this, "Bring me another chicken." Then he would ask for some tobacco, and even for a little money. It is probable that the better-paid Roman soldiers in our Lord's time did the same kind of thing; for an unarmed subject population cannot easily put a limit to the exactions of an armed man who plays the part of a cuckoo in a robin's nest.

More than one explanation has been given by commentators in different ages, as to why the genealogy in Matthew differs so completely from the genealogy in Luke. I think that Dr Heer, like Matthew Henry, has adopted the true explanation. St Matthew, having received the story of the Nativity from Joseph, gave also Joseph's genealogy, through which our Lord's claim to be the Messiah and the official descendant of David is asserted; for Matthew's aim in writing his Gospel was chiefly to convince his Jewish countrymen of this fact. Luke, on the other hand, gives us Mary's account of the Nativity, and therefore he gives us also Mary's genealogy. His chief aim was to convince his friend Theophilus and other Gentiles that Jesus of Nazareth was the Son of

God. Our Lord's claim to the Messiahship would have had very little weight with them. I cannot think that the story of the Virgin Mary's parents being named Joachim and Anne rests on any secure foundation. It is derived from a fabulous book called the *Protevangelium Jacobi* (which I have myself edited in its Syriac dress), and which, though embodying early traditions, was excluded from the list of canonical, and even true books, by the Decretum Gelasii in the sixth century, but upon which the whole worship of the Virgin Mary in the Roman Church rests. Anne may have been the name of Mary's mother, though it has obviously been suggested to the mind of the romancer, by the story of the prophet Samuel, or more probably of Susannah.

The Talmud tells us that the name of Mary's father was Heli.[1] Men, says Dr Heer, were often called the immediate fathers of their daughter's children. We can find more than

[1] Jerusalem, Talmud, Chagizgah, fol. 77, 4. Some Jewish scholars deny that our Lord's mother is meant in this passage. But I would ask, What other Mary could there be against whom their ancestors had such a violent hatred?

one instance of this for ourselves in the Old Testament. Athaliah was the daughter of Ahab and Jezebel, yet in 2 Kings viii. 26; 2 Chron. xxii. 2, she is called the daughter of Omri, who was Ahab's father. I love to think that our Lord was not an actual descendant of the gorgeous Solomon, nor of any Jewish crowned head excepting David, the sweet singer of Israel, whose poetic gift seems to have been inherited by the most blessed among women. No. He sprang from a line of more modest ancestors, amongst whom we find no kingly names save those of Zerubbabel and Salathiel, names which may possibly represent quite different people from those in 1 Chron.[1] and in Ezra. Possibly Mary may have been descended from a more consistently God-fearing stock than Joseph (see Zech. xii. 12). Justin Martyr[2] and Irenæus[3] both assume that the genealogy in Luke is that of Mary. Justin, indeed, tells us that amongst the Jews a man was often called the father of his

[1] 1 Chron. iii. 19.
[2] *Dial. cum Tryphone*, 43, 88, 100.
[3] Book iii. c. 22.

daughter's children (*Dial.* 43), and it is possible in reading Luke iii. 23 to shift the bracket and make the parenthesis begin with "as," and end with "Joseph." We should then read, "*And Jesus Himself was* (*beginning to be about thirty years old*, *being*, *as was supposed*, *the son of Joseph*,) *of Heli*, *of Matthat*," etc.

The Sinai text, with the Curetonian, the Diatessaron, and the Old Latin Codices e and f, omits the word ἀρχόμενος, "beginning" (to be). I do not see that this omission affects the main question. But if we take the phrase about our Lord's age, and about His being supposed to be the son of Joseph, as parenthetical, we have a distinct statement that Jesus was the son (or grandson) of Heli. Dr C. Vogt calls attention to the fact that this statement, "*And Jesus Himself was of Heli*," is expressed in precisely the same grammatical form as all the other phrases expressing sonship which follow it; thus, "Jesus Himself was of Heli, of Matthat, of Levi," etc. The word υἱός, "son," does not come into the true genealogy at all, but into the supposed one.

Our English translators ought not to have inserted the explanatory words "which was" into that genealogy at all.

It is a curious coincidence, though, of course, no proof, that some of our Lord's direct ancestors, according to Luke's genealogy, are referred to in the prophecy of Zechariah (Zech. xii. 12–14). After the statement that "they shall look on Him whom they have pierced," we are told that "the land shall mourn . . . the family of the house of David apart, and their wives apart; the family of the house of Nathan apart, and their wives apart; the family of the house of Levi apart, and their wives apart; the family of the house of Shimei apart, and their wives apart." These names are found in Luke's genealogy; the only doubtful one among them being that of Shimei, or Semei, which may, like some other Hebrew names, have been transliterated into a form which its bearer would hardly have recognised.

Dr Riggenbach[1] (quoted by Vogt, *Biblische*

[1] See *Theologische Studien und Kritiken* (1885), p. 584 *seqq.*

Studien, Band xii., Heft 2, p. 81) remarks that Luke's genealogy cannot possibly be that of Joseph, because, if it were, he would never have taken all value and interest out of it by prefixing to it the words *ὡς ἐνομίζετο*, "as was supposed." Luke, being a Greek by education, was anxious to show that Jesus is the Saviour of the world, not merely of the Hebrew nation. He therefore traces His descent from Adam rather than from Abraham. Dr Vogt's translation of Luke iii. 23, 24 does not differ much from my own. His use of the word "descended" seems to me a very happy one. It at least emphasises the distinction between *υἱός* and *τοῦ*, which are both good ways of expressing sonship.

Vogt's translation is—

"Und wirklich stammte er selber, dieser Jesus,—der zu Beginn seines öffentlichen Auftretens ungefähr dreissig Jahre zahlte, er, wie man meinte, Josephs Sohn—von Heli, von Matthat," usw.

"And actually he was descended, this Jesus —(who at the beginning of His public appearance was about thirty years old), he who was supposed to be Joseph's son—from Heli, from Matthat," etc.

I would suggest that in Luke's genealogy no man whose name is given is said to be the son of his predecessor on the list. We are only told that our Lord was descended from them all; for they all depend separately on the verb ἦν, "was." We may assume that the chronological succession is in the main correct; but quite possibly Zerubbabel and Salathiel ought to come into the list earlier than they do.

In chap. iv. ver. 17, we read, "*And they gave*," or rather, "*and he gave unto Him the book of Isaia the prophet, and He stood up for to read.*" Here the two clauses of the verse, and therefore the two acts, are transposed from what they are in other texts; the Sinai one narrating that our Lord did not rise till He was asked to read, by the book being put into His hands by the attendant of the synagogue.

In ver. 18, instead of "to set at liberty them that are bruised," we have "*to send away the contrite with forgiveness*," or "*to assure the contrite of forgiveness.*" We are uncertain about the verb; "to send away" and "to assure" being differentiated in Syriac only by a tiny dot, now hidden in the palimpsest by a heavy line of the upper writing. But whichever it may be, it is an improvement on the tautology of the usual text. The Peshiṭta has a reading not unlike this, and there we have distinctly the verb "to send away." The reading of the Sinaiticus, Vaticanus, and Alexandrinus, ἀποστεῖλαι τεθραυσμένους ἐν ἀφέσει, might be translated thus, if ἁμαρτιῶν be implied.

In ver. 27 we read, "*And not one of them was cleansed, save a Syrian.*" Naaman is not mentioned.

In ver. 29 we are told that the people of Nazareth "*led Him to the hill Faras whereon their city was built, so that they might hang Him.*" The word "hang" is evidently a mistake, the Syriac translator having taken κρημνίσαι for κρεμάσαι. And "Faras," as Wellhausen has pointed out, is the Greek ὀφρὺς, "eyebrow" or "cliff."

In Luke iv. 44, v. 1, we read, "*And He*

preached in the synagogues of Judæa, and in the crowd which was crushing that it might hear from Him the word of God." We find "Judæa" instead of "Galilee" in Codd. Sinaiticus, Vaticanus, and in four other Greek and some Coptic MSS.

In Luke v. 26 we read, after the miracle on the paralytic, "*And astonishment took hold of them and they were all glorifying God, and saying, We have seen glorious, great things to-day.*"

Luke vi. 1 is not extant in the Old Syriac Version; both the Sinai and the Curetonian MSS. having lost the leaf which had it. Here our Authorised Version follows the evidently corrupt reading of Codd. A, C, D, and twelve other Greek uncials, the Peshiṭta, the Latin Vulgate, etc. The Revisers have attempted, not very successfully, to explain this away. These beforementioned codices contain the quite unintelligible Greek word δευτεροπρώτῳ.

Ἐγένετο δὲ ἐν σαββάτῳ δευτεροπρώτῳ διαπορεύεσθαι αὐτὸν διὰ τῶν σπορίμων· καὶ ἔτιλλον οἱ μαθηταὶ αὐτοῦ τοὺς στάχυας καὶ ἤσθιον, ψώχοντες ταῖς χερσί.

It ought to be, "And it came to pass on the second Sabbath early in the morning, that He went through the corn-fields; and His disciples plucked the ears of corn, rubbing them in their hands."

πρώτῳ has probably been substituted for πρωΐ by the copyist of a very early MS., perhaps even of Luke's autograph, through a process which I hope to explain in discussing the text of John i. 41, where I detected an exactly similar mistake, with the help of the Sinai Palimpsest. On that occasion Dr Burkitt suggested that I should look at the Greek of Luke vi. 1.

In Luke vi. 20, 21 we have, "*Blessed are the poor: for theirs is the kingdom of heaven. Blessed are they that hunger now: for they shall be satisfied. Blessed are they that weep now: for they shall laugh.*"

Codex B alone of the Palestinian Syriac Version has "theirs" instead of "yours" in the first of these beatitudes, and "they" instead of "ye" in the second.

In Luke vi. 24 there is a curious mistake in the Syriac text. The word παράκλησις has two meanings in Greek, literally "invitation," and metaphorically "consolation." So the Syriac translator says, "*But woe unto you rich! for ye have received your invitation.*"

In Luke vi. 25, "Woe unto you that are full now, for ye shall hunger" is omitted.

In Luke vi. 33 our Lord asks His disciples, "*And if ye do good to him who doeth good to you, what is your kindness?*"

In Luke vi. 35 we read, "*Do not cut off the hope of any*," or "*Do not cease hope of man*," instead of "never despairing."

And in Luke vi. 40, "*There is no disciple who is perfect as his master in teaching.*"

In Luke vi. 48, in the parable of the man who built his house on the rock, we read, "*and when there were floods, and the rivers were full, they beat upon that house, and could not shake it.*"

In Luke vii. 24 "into the wilderness" is omitted.

In Luke vii. 29 we have a reading which may possibly be the original one: "*And all the people and the publicans that heard, justified them-*

selves to God, who were baptized with the baptism of John."

In Luke viii. 19 we are told that "*His mother and His brothers came to Him, and could not see, and were waiting because of the crowd.*"

In Luke viii. 41 the name of the ruler of the synagogue whose daughter was healed is given as Joarish or Juarish. This is considered by Dr Burkitt as a blemish on the Sinai text; but it seems to me that it is a natural Semitic and actual Arabic diminutive of the Old Testament name Jair, after the analogy of "kelb," "kulaib," the final consonant "sh" being a common Greek appendix to foreign names. If we are in the habit of calling one of our Scotch friends "Jamie," we need not be surprised if his French acquaintances should address him respectfully as "Monsieur Jacques." To me this is an additional proof that the Old Syriac Version came into being on Palestinian soil.

An omission of the Sinai text in Luke viii. 43 makes us suspect that the Evangelist did not really record the failures of his professional brethren; and that to Mark alone are we indebted for the information that the woman who sought our Lord's help after His departure from the country of the Gadarenes, "had spent all her living upon physicians, and was nothing bettered, but rather grew worse." Some too zealous scribe has evidently filled Luke's text in the Greek MSS. with a phrase of Mark's.

Luke viii. 45 reads, "*Our Master, the multitude throng and press Thee, and sayest Thou, Who touched Me?*" (with Codd. Alexandrinus, Ephræmi, Bezæ, Brixianus, and other Greek and Latin MSS., the Curetonian, the Peshiṭta, and our Authorised Version).

And Luke ix. 37, "*And in that day when they were come down from the mountain,*" instead of "And it came to pass, *on the next day,*" etc. (almost with the Curetonian, and possibly with Codd. Bezæ, Veronensis, and those Latin MSS. which say *per diem*), or *in illa die.*

The great painter Raphael must surely have believed this to be the true reading. For he has depicted the scene of the nine disciples trying to cast the demon out of a boy, at the foot of a mountain, whilst our Lord is being transfigured on its summit, in the presence of Moses, Elias, and the other three disciples.

The scene is thus described by the father of the boy (ver. 39), "*And a spirit cometh to him suddenly, and it throweth him down, and chastiseth him; and he foameth, and it hardly departeth from him, when it hath bruised him*" (with the Curetonian).

In Luke ix. 45, "*and they were afraid about this saying*," instead of "to ask about."

And in ix. 61, "*but first let me go and tell it to them of my house, and I will come*," instead of "to bid farewell" (with the Curetonian and some Old Latin MSS.).

In x. 1, "*And after these things he appointed of his disciples other seventy-two* (with Codd. Vaticanus and Bezæ, some Old Latin MSS., and almost with the Curetonian).

And in x. 16, "*He that heareth you, heareth Me; and He who wrongeth you, wrongeth Him that sent Me; and he that heareth Me, heareth Him that sent Me*." This is somewhat like the readings of Codex Bezæ and of the Curetonian, but it is not exactly like either of them.

In ver. 22, "*All things are delivered to Me from the Father; and who knoweth the Son, except the Father? and who knoweth the Father, except the Son, and he to whom the Son will reveal Him?*"

In ver. 35, "*And at the dawn of the day he took out two pence*" (with the Curetonian and the Peshiṭta). This is in accordance with the early start usually made by natives of the East when they are on a journey.

In Luke x. 41 we have simply, "*Martha, Martha, Mary hath chosen for herself the good part, which shall not be taken away from her.*" "Thou art anxious and troubled about many things: but one thing is needful," being omitted (with Codd. Vercellensis and Veronensis). Codex Bezæ omits the second clause of this only. It is pleasing to imagine that our Lord did not really rebuke the anxiety of a careful housewife. He only meant her to understand that there is something of far higher moment than our daily bread. The reading of the Sinaiticus and Vaticanus is, "there is need of little except of one thing" (Sin. ὀλίγων δὲ ἐστιν χρεία ἢ ἑνός).

In Luke xi. 2–4 the Lord's Prayer is thus given: "*Father, Hallowed be Thy name, and Thy kingdom come. And give us the continual bread of every day. And forgive us our sins; and we also, we forgive every one who is indebted to us. And lead us not into temptation.*"

In Luke xi. 13 we are told about the Father being willing to give "*good things* (not "the Holy Spirit") *to them that ask Him.*"

In Luke xi. 36 we have a very curious reading: "*Therefore also Thy body, when there is in it no lamp that shines, is dark; thus while thy lamp is shining, it gives light to thee.*" This is something like the Latin Codex Brixianus, which Tischendorf says has here a corrupt reading.

And in Luke xi. 53, "*And as He said these things against them in the sight* (Syriac, "in the eye") *of all the people, He began to be displeasing to the scribes and to the Pharisees; and they were disputing with Him about many things, and were seeking to lay hold of an accusation against Him*" (almost with Codex Bezæ, some Old Latin MSS., and the Curetonian).

In Luke xii. 27 we are told to "*Consider*

the lilies; how they spin not, and weave not," instead of "they toil not, neither do they spin" (with Codd. Bezæ and Vercellensis, and the Curetonian). Here we detect in other MSS. the hand of a harmoniser, who has obviously tried to make the text of St Luke agree with that of St Matthew, and if we assume that this reading be the true one, he has, in so doing, obscured a very appropriate allusion to the sequence of those processes by which our clothes come into existence.

Dr Arnold Meyer has pointed out that the verb used in Luke xii. 46 and in Matt. xxiv. 51 in all the Syriac versions, *palleg*, has the primary meaning of "cut in pieces," and the secondary one of "appoint to some one his portion."[1] If we suppose that our Lord used it in the primary sense, the difficulty as to how the man survived so trying a process becomes insoluble. But if we take it in the secondary one, we must assume that the Evangelist, whilst

[1] Cf. *Jesv Muttersprache*, p. 115. Dr Meyer attributes these meanings to the *Afel* form of the verb. But they belong also to the form *Pael.*

investigating about all these things, and writing them down carefully in Greek for the benefit of Theophilus, misunderstood a Syriac idiom by taking it too literally. The translation would then be: "*and shall allot his portion, and shall place him* [*or it*] *with the unfaithful,*" etc.

This parable, as Dr Rendel Harris has pointed out, is possibly taken from the story of Achikar, which belongs to the Pseudepigraphy of the Old Testament, and just missed getting into the canonical Apocrypha. Achikar had a wicked and ungrateful nephew named Nadan, who behaved in precisely the same way as this bad servant did, and who met with a similar fate.

CHAPTER VII

VARIANTS IN LUKE—*continued*

In Luke xiii. 19 we are told of the grain of mustard seed, that "*it grew up and became a tree, and the fowls of the air nested in its branches.*"

In Luke xiii. 35 we have, "*Behold, your house is forsaken,*" instead of "is left unto you desolate" (almost with the Sinaiticus, the Vaticanus, the Alexandrinus, and many other ancient Greek MSS.; also with the Old Latin Friuli Lectionary). If this be the original reading, it perhaps means that God was about to withdraw His special favour from the Jewish nation.

In Luke xiv. 12, "*When thou makest a supper, call not thy friends, nor thy brethren, nor thy rich neighbours,*" etc.

It is supposed that perhaps behind the Greek of this passage there lies a Semitic idiom, by which in the first limb of a sentence the negative is made stronger than the speaker really intended it to be, in order to make more emphatic the statement in the second limb. Thus the true translation would be, "*When thou makest a supper, call not only thy friends,*" etc. Our Lord, who attended so many social gatherings, did not surely intend to forbid hospitality to our equals as well as to our poorer neighbours. For examples of this idiom, see Jer. vii. 22, John xii. 44, and Dr Hommel's papers in the *Expository Times* for July and August 1900. This idiom is, of course, not peculiar to the Sinai Palimpsest.

Other examples in the New Testament are: "Labour not (only) for the meat that perisheth, but for that meat which endureth unto everlasting life" (John vi. 27).

"He that believeth on Me, believeth not (only) on Me, but on Him that sent Me" (John xii. 44).

"Whose adorning, let it not be (only) that

outward adorning of plaiting the hair, and of wearing of gold, or of putting on of apparel; but the hidden man of the heart, in that which is not corruptible, a meek and quiet spirit, which is in the sight of God of great price" (1 Pet. iii. 3, 4).

The passage in Luke's Gospel is thus brought into harmony with St Peter's injunction to "use hospitality one to another without grudging" (1 Pet. iv. 9), and with St Paul's, to be "given to hospitality" (Rom. xii. 13).

Our Lord's saying, reported in John xii. 44, becomes comprehensible only by the insertion of "only." The existence of this idiom, which is very common in Arabic, is a striking example of the misconceptions which may arise when we neglect to compare Scripture with Scripture. I well recollect, that in my childhood, we were acquainted with more than one good lady who thought that the wearing of ornaments, or of flowers and feathers, if not actually sinful, showed an indifference to spiritual things, or was the evidence of a giddy and thoughtless mind. But when I learnt French,

8

and read Michelet's delightful books, *L'Oiseau*, and *L'Insecte*, I began to see that the Creator who gives to the birds their brilliant plumes, and to the butterflies their delicate wings, especially in "the spring-time, the only pretty ring-time," cannot frown on His human children adorning themselves occasionally to please each other. Even the passage in Isaiah, on which our critical friends relied so much, the passage about the wimples, and the bracelets, and the round tires like the moon, does not condemn these things as actually sinful; but merely prophesies that they shall disappear in the stress of national misfortune.

In Luke xiv. 13 the Sinai text has the list of guests longer than usual: "*call the poor, and the blind, and the lame and the afflicted, and the outcast, and many others.*"

In Luke xv. 13 we are told that the younger son went into a far country, "*and there squandered his substance, because he was living wastefully with harlots*" (with the Curetonian). This is perhaps an addition from ver. 30.

When the elder son returned, he heard

"*piping and symphony*," instead of "music and dancing." The Curetonian Version is here deficient; but we observe with some interest that the Peshiṭta and the Palestinian Syriac also omit "dancing." Greek and Roman ideas on the subject are to this day very different from Arab ones. Nothing can be more beautiful than the open-air dances of maidens which we have witnessed on the sward of Parnassus or of the Peloponnesus. The men of the village look on and listen to the song which accompanies the gliding movements of the girls; choosing mayhap their brides as they watch. Moslem ideas of dancing are confined to the performances of the nautch-girl and the "'alimah."

The word *συμφωνία* is said to refer to a primitive kind of music resembling that produced by the Scottish bagpipe, or the Italian *pifara*.

In Luke xvi. 1–9 we have a remarkable variant. Instead of "Take thy bond, and sit down quickly, and write fifty," we have, "*And he* (*i.e.* the steward) *sat down quickly, and wrote them fifty*." Also in ver. 8, "*And he sat down immediately [and] wrote them fourscore.*" At a period of the world's history when ordinary folk could not read, it seems natural that the steward should do the writing himself.

And some of the difficulties in this parable might disappear if we could suppose that the steward was sacrificing his own unjust gains, and leaving the debtors to pay only what was due to his lord, when he remitted the full half of their debt.

The practice of tax-gatherers, stewards, and others exacting twice as much as they ought to get, and then putting half of it into their own pockets, is still common in the Turkish empire. It was the earthly lord of the steward who thought that he had done wisely.

In Luke xvi. 11 our Lord asks: "*Who will commit to you the truth?*" (not "the true riches"). The Peshiṭta also has this variant.

In Luke xvi. 16 we read, "*and every man presseth into it.*" The Syriac word does not imply violence. This clause is omitted in Codex Sinaiticus. Codex Vercellensis has "all hasten into it."

In Luke xvi. 20 Lazarus is "*a certain poor man*," instead of "a certain beggar." And as such he seems more entitled to our respect. We begin to entertain a faint hope that the Charity Organisation Society would not have improved him away. It is the same in ver. 22. The Greek πτωχὸς may mean a beggar, but I have heard the Arabic equivalent of the Syriac *meskîn* (Fr. *mesquin*) applied to a person who was simply unhappy. The Peshiṭta, the Palestinian Syriac, and the Coptic have the equivalent of *pauper*, the Curetonian being deficient. Some Old Latin MSS. have *pauper* and some *mendicus*.

In Luke xvi. 25 "Son" is omitted in the reply of Abraham. This may perhaps be significant.

In Luke xvii. 10, "*So likewise ye, when ye shall have done all those things which are commanded you, say ye, We are servants: what was our duty to do we have done.*" The word "unprofitable" is here omitted. (Note in connection with Matt. vi. 7 that the Syriac word for it in the Peshiṭta is *baṭila*). Good servants are very far from being unprofitable. So we suspect that the word has crept into the Greek codices through the excessive humility of some ancient scribe. God surely does not despise our obedience.

This variant is believed to be the original reading by several distinguished scholars, including Dr Frederick Blass and Dr Wellhausen. It has no corroboration, as yet, in any other MS. or ancient writing, but it almost contains its own credentials. It is also a source of great encouragement to many believers to be told that they may be efficient co-workers with their Heavenly Master.

In Luke xvii. 21 we have, "*for behola the kingdom of God is amongst you*," not "within you."

And in ver. 24, "*For as the lightning lighteneth from end to end of heaven, so shall be the day of the Son of man.*" This is a little more concise than the usual ending.

In Luke xviii. 5 the unjust judge says: "*I will avenge her, lest at the last she should come and take hold of me.*" We cannot attempt to explain this, unless he was haunted by a dread of what the widow could do, the more fearsome because it was vague.

In Luke xix. 12 "A certain nobleman" is called "*A certain man, the son of a great family.*"

In Luke xix. 28 we are told, "*And when He had said these things, they went out from there. And as He was going up to Jerusalem and had reached Bethphage and Bethany,*" etc.

In Luke xix. 39 we have, "*Good teacher, rebuke thy disciples, that they shout not*" (almost with the Curetonian).

In Luke xx. 16, 17 we find, instead of, "And when they heard it, they said, God forbid. But He looked upon them, and said, What then is this that is written," etc., we have, "*When they heard these things, they knew certainly that He spake this parable about them. But He beheld them, and said, What is this then that is written,*" etc.

Luke xx. 24 has "*Why tempt ye Me? Show Me a penny*" (with our Authorised Version).

And Luke xx. 34, "*The children of this world beget and go on begetting, and marry and are given in marriage.*" (A reading somewhat like this is found in Codex Bezæ, some of the Old Latin MSS., and the Curetonian.)

Luke xx. 46 reports that our Lord said: "*Beware of the scribes, which desire to walk in the porches,*" instead of "in long robes," *i.e.* στοαῖς for στολαῖς, as in Mark xii. 38 (with the Curetonian).

In Luke xxi. 25, 26 we are told, "*And there shall be signs in the sun, and in the moon, and in the stars; and distress upon the earth, and weakness of the hands of the nations; and the voice of the sea, and shaking; and men's souls shall go out for fear of what is about to come on the earth; and the powers of heaven shall shake*" (almost like the Curetonian and the Peshiṭta).

And about the fig-tree, and all the trees, in Luke xxi. 29, "*When they begin to shoot forth and yield their fruit*" (with Codex Bezæ and the Old Latin Friuli Lectionary, which, however, omit "shoot forth," and the Curetonian).

We learn from the Encyclopædia that "the fig-trees in Asiatic Turkey usually bear two crops: one in the early summer from the buds of the last year ; the other in the autumn from those on the spring growth ; the latter forms the chief harvest.

This statement throws some light on the story of the barren fig-tree in Mark xi. 12–14.

In Luke xxii. the story of the Last Supper is differently arranged from what it is in our English Revised Version. The sequence of the verses being 16, 19, 20*a*, 17, 20*b*, 18, 21. The repetition of our Lord's giving the cup is therefore non-existent. I give the passage from my own translation.

In ver. 15, "*He said unto them, With desire I have desired to eat the passover with you before I suffer:* 16 *for I say unto you, I will not any more eat thereof, until the kingdom of God be perfected.* 19 *And He took bread, and gave thanks over it, and brake, and gave unto them saying, This is My body which I give for you : thus do in remembrance of Me.* 20 *And after they had supped, He took the cup,* 17 *and gave thanks over it, and said, Take this, share it among yourselves.* 20 *This is My blood, the new testament.* 18 *For I say unto you, that henceforth I will not drink of this fruit, until the kingdom of God shall come.* 21 *But nevertheless, behold, the hand of My betrayer is with Me on the table.*"

We leave it to the judgment of our readers as to whether this does not appear to be an approach to the original form of the passage. Codex Bezæ and some Old Latin MSS. omit ver. 20 altogether, with part of ver. 19, thus avoiding the repetition, but making the taking of the cup precede that of the bread. The order in the Old Latin Codex Veronensis is a remarkable one. It is vers. 16, 19, 17, 18, 21, 22, 23, etc. Here the taking of the bread precedes that of the cup, and there is no repetition.

The Curetonian, being the sister manuscript to the Sinaitic, or as we may now more properly call it, the Syro-Antiochene Palimpsest, has the narrative in a precisely similar order; only it omits two phrases: "after they had supped," and "This is My blood, the new testament." The latter may perhaps more properly belong to Matt. xxvi. 28 or to Mark xiv. 24, and the former to 1 Cor. xi. 25. This is exactly the kind of narrative which was likely to suffer from the hand of a harmoniser. As it was so frequently read in the Communion service, the early Christians would naturally desire to have it as complete as possible ; and they would not heed the fact that they were obscuring the characteristic touches of the four Evangelists, and of our Lord's own revelation to St Paul.

We must never forget, in considering this subject, that there were four cups passed round to the guests at a Passover feast.

The Sinai text agrees with Codex Vaticanus, Codex Alexandrinus, and the Old Latin Codex Brixianus in omitting

Luke xxii. 43, 44.—"And there appeared unto Him an angel from heaven, strengthening Him. And, being in an agony, He prayed more earnestly ; and His sweat became as it were great drops of blood falling down upon the ground." This has long been considered a doubtful passage.

In Luke xxii. 68 our Lord says : "*And if I ask you, ye will not give Me an answer, nor even let Me go*" (with Codd. Alexandrinus and

Bezæ, the Curetonian, the Peshiṭta, and some Old Latin MSS.).

In Luke xxiii. 6, 7 we read, "*But when Pilate heard them say that He was of Galilee,*" instead of "But when Pilate heard it, he asked whether the man were a Galilean."

And in xxiii. 9, "*Then he questioned with Him in cunning words*" (with the Curetonian).

We next have an important omission in vers. 10, 11, 22, for the statement, "And the chief priests and the scribes stood, vehemently accusing Him. And Herod with his soldiers set Him at nought, and mocked Him, and arraying Him in gorgeous apparel, sent Him back to Pilate. And Herod and Pilate became friends with each other that very day; for before they were at enmity between themselves," is not there.

In Luke xxiii. 15 Pilate says: "*No, nor yet Herod, for I sent Him to him.*" This seems more natural than the reading of the Revised Version, "for he sent Him back unto us" (with the Curetonian, the Peshiṭta, almost with Codex Bezæ, and some Old Latin MSS.).

Ver. 15 continues, "*nothing that is worthy of*

death did he find against Him, nor has anything worthy of death been done by Him" (with the Curetonian).

In ver. 18 the people cry, "*Take away this man, and release Bar-Abba; he who because of wicked deeds and murder was cast into prison.*" Neither here nor in Mark xv. 7 does our codex make any mention of an insurrection.

Ver. 17 comes after ver. 19, "*And Pilate was wont to release one prisoner unto them at the feast*" (with Codex Bezæ and the Curetonian). Codd. Vaticanus, Alexandrinus, and the Old Latin Vercellensis omit ver. 17 altogether.

In Luke xxiii. 20 we read, "*And again Pilate called them, and said unto them, because he was willing to release Jesus, Whom will ye that I release unto you?*" The question is found also in Matt. xxvii. 17, and it seems also necessary for the sense.

And in ver. 23, "*And their voice prevailed, and the chief priests were with them*" (with the Curetonian and the Peshiṭta). Codd. Alexandrinus, Bezæ, and Brixianus have "their voices and those of the chief priests."

And in ver. 25, "*And he released unto them him who for murder and wicked deeds was cast into prison.*" There is still no mention of insurrection or sedition.

The most beautiful of our Lord's sayings, usually found in xxiii. 34, "And Jesus said, Father, forgive them; for they know not what they do," is omitted. Westcott and Hort have put this in brackets, and it is omitted in Codex Vaticanus, Codex Bezæ, and several Old Latin MSS. But Codd. Sinaiticus and Alexandrinus, the Peshiṭta, and all the other Syriac versions, including the Curetonian MS., retain it.

Dr Hjelt considers the omission of this saying a strong proof of the antiquity of the Sinai text. It is in the Diatessaron, and if the Old Syriac Version had been made subsequently to the promulgation of that Harmony, all Syriac Christians would have resented the omission of a saying with which they were, after the year A.D. 170 at latest, already familiar. The only way in which we can account for its absence from the Sinai text is, that when the translation which lies behind that document was made, the most gracious of our Lord's sayings was as yet unknown.

In Luke xxiii. 36, "offering Him vinegar" is omitted (with the Curetonian).

In vers. 37, 38 we read that the soldiers also mocked Him, and they were coming near Him, "*saying, Hail to Thee! If Thou be the king of the Jews, save Thyself*" (with Codex Bezæ and the Curetonian).

Ver. 37 adds, "*And they placed also on His heaa a crown of thorns,*" *i.e.* whilst He was on the cross (with Codex Bezæ and the Curetonian).

In ver. 39 there is an important variant. We were not aware of its existence till my sixth (and I hope final) visit to Sinai in 1906. Then, with the help of the re-agent, I got two words which the first transcriber could not have seen. It reads thus in the speech of one of the malefactors who was crucified, who blasphemed against Him, saying unto Him, "*Art not Thou the Saviour? Save Thyself to-day, and also us.*"

I am absolutely sure of the word "Saviour."

Nothing is more common in Semitic speech than the use of a noun and a verb together which are derived from the same root. And we can hear a distinct echo of the word "*to-day*," though it was flung at Him in a time of reproach, in our Lord's kind answer to the other malefactor, "*To-day shalt thou be with Me in Paradise*" (ver. 43).

The repentant thief's petition, "*Lord, remember me when Thou comest in Thy kingdom*," is surely a better translation of the Greek than "into Thy kingdom," which we have in the Authorised Version. The Sinai text in this verse agrees with our Revised Version, and with the Curetonian, the Peshiṭta, the Veronensis, and several other Old Latin MSS.

In ver. 48 we are told, "*And all those who had ventured there, and saw what happened, smote upon their breasts, saying, Woe to us, what hath befallen us! Woe to us for our sins!*" (with the Curetonian and partly with the apocryphal Gospel of Peter).

In Luke xxiv. 1 we read, "*and they brought what they had prepared, and other women came with them*," that is, in addition to the women who came with Him from Galilee: *cf.* xxiii. 55 (with Codex Bezæ, Codex Brixianus, the Curetonian, Peshiṭta, and the Palestinian Syriac).

Luke xxiv. 10 has, "and Mary, the *daughter* of James" (with the Curetonian and with A and B of the Palestinian Syriac, *i.e.* with two MSS. which were found by Dr Rendel Harris and myself in the same box with the palimpsest); as in Matt. xxvii. 56; Mark xv. 47, xvi. 1.

In Luke xxiv. 11 we are told that Mary the Magdalene, and Joanna, and Mary the daughter of James, appeared in the eyes of the eleven apostles as "*if they had spoken these words from their wonder*," instead of "as idle talk" (with the Curetonian). This is not the last time that a true story has been disbelieved because it was told by a woman.

In Luke xxiv. 17 we are told that Jesus said to the two disciples on the road to Emmaus, "*What are these words which ye talk of whilst ye are sad?*" Here we have sixteen words instead of the twenty-four of the Revised

Version (with the Curetonian and some Old Latin MSS.).

In Luke xxiv. 29 we read about these two disciples, "*And they began to entreat Him that He would be with them, because it was nearly dark. And He went in with them as if He would tarry with them*" (with the Curetonian).

In Luke xxiv. 41 we read, "*and while until that time they had not believed from their joy and from their fear, and they were astonished. He said again unto them,*" etc.

The Curetonian is defective from ver. 43.

And in Luke xxiv. 51, 52, "*And while He blessed them, He was lifted up from them, and was carried up into heaven*" (with the Curetonian and the Peshiṭta). "And they worshipped Him" is omitted (with Codex Bezæ and some Old Latin MSS.).

It will be observed that there are more variations between the Revised Version and the text of the palimpsest in the Gospel of Luke than in the two preceding ones. We do not know if this lends any support to Dr Blass' theory of two recensions of this Gospel having been made by Luke himself, one which he sent to Theophilus, and one for the Christians in Rome.

It is in the Gospel of John, however, that variants of the Sinai text have enabled us to explain the greatest number of obscure passages.

CHAPTER VIII

VARIANTS IN JOHN

In the first chapter of John's Gospel vers. 1–24 are completely wanting in the Sinai Palimpsest, because a leaf of it has been lost. We know, however, almost what they are in the Old Syriac, *i.e.* in the second-century translation from which both the Sinai and the Curetonian MSS. have sprung, or perhaps I should say, of which both are the legitimate descendants. It therefore cannot be out of place for me to notice two important variants which have been preserved to us by the Curetonian MS., surmising at the same time that they probably were also at one time in the Sinai one. The first of these variants depends entirely on the punctuation of ver. 3. If we take our Authorised English Version, and transfer the full stop from after the last word in that verse, the word "made" to the word "made" which occurs as the third word before it, we find that the passage will read thus:

"*All things were made by Him, and without Him was not anything made. That which was made in Him was life, and the life was the light of men.*" This variant, to which Dr Burkitt attaches some importance, is interesting, but I do not see that it has any appreciable effect on the meaning. Very different is the variant in ver. 13. It says: "*Who* (pl.) *was born, not in blood, and not of the will of the body,*" etc., "*nor of the will of man, but of God.*"

Dr Burkitt considers that the mistake here must be in "was born." A mistake there is, for the nominative to "was born," *i.e.* "who," is in the plural. Dr Burkitt allows that some MSS. of the Peshiṭta have a similar reading. The late Dr Frederick Blass, of Halle, on the other hand, considered that ἐγεννήθη is the true reading, and that it is appropriately followed by καὶ ὁ λόγος in ver. 14. "And the Word was made flesh" (in Syriac, "became a body"). Both readings state an actual fact, and while it may be difficult to decide which we prefer, we should not forget that the copy of the Gospel used by St Augustine in the fourth century must have said, "*qui natus est.*" No one can now confidently maintain that the Fourth Gospel contains no allusion to the Virgin-birth.

In ver. 28 the Sinai Palimpsest says: "*These things He spake in Beth'abara beyond Jordan, where John was baptizing.*" Our English Revisers have followed all the Greek uncials in adopting "*Bethany,*" but the best of the Greek cursives have *Beth'abara.* How shall we decide between them?

The Bethany where Lazarus dwelt cannot be intended, for it is not beyond Jordan. It is not far from the summit of the Mount of Olives, on the side which looks towards the Dead Sea, and it therefore cannot be seen from Jerusalem. Professor Bacon, of Yale University, America, identifies it with a village which he discovered up among the hills of the eastern side of the Jordan valley; a village whose modern name is Bottony. I would, however, suggest that both names may have been appropriately given

Beth 'abara = Bethany beyond Jordan.—John i. 28.

[*To face page* 135.

Dr Burkitt cannot therefore have got the two words from my photograph. He copied it from the MS. as ܝܘܡܐ ܘ[ܗܘܐ], and the MS., during my sixth visit to Sinai in 1906, has told me a different story.

I touched the margin with the re-agent. To my great surprise, there came up clearly the word ܠܫܦܪܗ, "at the dawn." The next word needed no chemical treatment, for even in 1892 it reproduced itself in my photograph as ܕܝܘܡܐ, "of the day."

I communicated this, along with other emendations, shortly after my return home, to several Syriac scholars. It attracted no particular attention, however, till quite lately. As the sheets of my new edition of the Sinai Gospels were passing through the press, I printed on the page containing John i. 41 corroborations which I had found in the published text of two Old Latin MSS., the Codex Veronensis (*b*):

> "Inuenit autem mane fratrem Ṣimonem et dicit illi: inuenimus Messiam."

and the Codex Palatinus (*e*):

"Et mane inuenit fratrem suum simonem et ait illi inuenimus messia."

It becomes at once evident that behind the Syriac of the Sinai Palimpsest, and behind the Latin of *b* and *e*, stood the same Greek word πρωΐ, which an early copyist mistook for πρῶτον. Hence we have "Andrew first findeth his brother Simon, and saith unto him," etc.

That the new reading is a good one goes almost without saying. Read vers. 40, 41, either in the English version or in the Greek text, substituting προΐ for πρῶτον, or "at the dawn of the day," *i.e.* "in the morning," for "first," and you will see that the chronological sequence becomes correct. "On that day," would be hardly natural; for if the meeting between the brothers took place some considerable time after the tenth hour, the word "evening" would have been used. Dr Nestle at once advised me to ascertain if there is not a similar reading in the Old Latin Codex Usserianus (r_1). I examined the text of Dr

Abbott's edition (1884), and found that the page which contains John i. 41 is imperfect, the first syllable of every line having disappeared, but before "fratrem suum" stands printed the letter *e*, showing that the missing word was *mane*, not *primum*. I thereupon wrote to Professor Wilkins of Trinity College, Dublin, requesting him to examine the manuscript, and to see if he could not detect any further trace of *mane*.

Professor Wilkins did so, in company with the editor, Dr Abbott. To their great regret they found that the *e* has disappeared, the edge of the leaf being very crumbly. But Dr Abbott is certain that it *was* there when he copied it. He formed no theory as to what word it stood for.

How did a copyist mistake πρωΐ for πρῶτον? At first we thought that there might have been a contraction (either in the original or in an early copy), which was wrongly expanded into πρῶτον or πρῶτος. I imagined that the ι of πρωΐ might have been written so close beneath the ω, as to be mistaken for a τ. But I am told that *iota subscriptum* is never found in early MSS.

Dr Wilkins has made the plausible suggestion that the copyist who made the mistake read the dots over an uncial ϊ as the upper stroke of a τ. Having once written πρωτ, he was almost obliged to add ον to make sense out of it.

If the reading πρωΐ be in truth the original one, some very interesting questions occur to us. (1) Was the Sacred Autograph written in an uncial script, or in a cursive? Papyrus and vellum would doubtless be costly. The Evangelists and the Apostles were men of slender means; it is therefore permissible to think that if they used uncials, these must have been very small ones.

(2) If so curious a mistake as πρῶτον for πρωΐ crept into the Gospel text before the fourth century, may not the same kind of accident account for small discrepancies between the four records of our Lord's life? and may there not be similar mistakes still undetected in the text of the Gospels?

It must be remembered that Codex Veronensis and Codex Palatinus both belong to either the fourth or the fifth century. Their claim to a high antiquity is therefore quite as good as that of the Sinaiticus and the Vaticanus; and they are translations into Latin from still older MSS. not now extant. The same may be said of the Syriac Palimpsest on Mount Sinai, which is probably the earliest translation of the Gospels into any language. It is indeed marvellous that we should thus be able to get behind the oldest of Greek texts, and to detect its slight corruptions.

But how does this affect the question of inspiration? If we believe that the New Testament was dictated, word for word, by the Holy Spirit, it would of course be fatal. But such verbal dictation is out of harmony with God's other ways of working. His gifts to man are, as I have already said, like pure water springing up in the mountains, or like the pure air which man has the power to preserve pure, or to taint. No special providence watched over the copyists. Both the Old and the New Testaments are records of the revelation of Himself which God made to man gradually, as man was able to receive it. Our faith in its moral teaching is therefore not shaken by any mistakes of copyists, nor even by mistakes, if there are any, of the inspired Recorders.

There are some men who expect absolute accuracy from the Protomartyr Stephen, quite forgetting that he spoke in the midst of a wild and angry crowd, most of whom held in their hands the stones which they were impatient to throw at his head. And the men who copied the Gospels did not always work in the seclusion of a college library, nor even in that of a monastic cell. They were doubtless, many of them, those of whom the world was not worthy; who, we are told in the Epistle to the Hebrews, dwelt in dens and caves of the earth. Possibly, in the second and the third century, the blood-stained sheep-skin cloak of some martyr scribe was carefully turned into parchment, for the reception of those words of life which its owner had died to preserve for us.

To this the following note was added by Dr Wilkins :—

"With regard to πρωΐ versus πρῶτον in John i. 41, it is interesting to note that in the *Odyssey* (xxiv. 28) πρῶϊ has been restored instead of πρῶτα, the vulgar reading, by Kayser, Ameis, La Roche, Faesi, and Monro. This is a case very closely parallel with ours."

"I think the autograph may have been written in such small and very neat uncials as those of the papyrus of Hyperides, of which Dr Kenyon gives a facsimile in Plate II. of his 'Classical Texts, from Papyri in the British Museum, with autotype facsimiles of MSS.' (1891), and which he dates as '*very early, and perhaps of the second century* B.C.' There, in the middle column, in the second and third lines (*et passim*), you will find *iota* and *tau* written thus :

ι (like a J) τ (like a J),

"the little toes turned westward in each case being exactly similar, so that πρωι and πρωτον might easily be mistaken."

"*If such a dainty-toed iota had two dots written above it, it would pass for a tau anywhere.*"

"Of course, defenders of πρῶτον could easily say that the Sinai Palimpsest and the three Latin Codices omitted τον after πρω by an error of haplography or ablepsia. But πρωϊ is the harder reading, and therefore the more likely to be original. And πρωϊ will account for the variants πρῶτος and πρῶτον; the scribe of ℵ, finding what he mistook for πρωτ, gave it a termination in agreement with οὗτος, the subject of the verb; while the scribe of A gave it a termination in agreement with τὸν ἀδελφόν, the object of the verb."

In John ii. 24, 25 we read, "*But our Lord did not trust Himself to them, and needed not that any should testify about the work of man: for He knew the heart in man what it is.*"

And in John iii. 6, "*And that which is born of the spirit is spirit; because God is a living Spirit.*" The Curetonian and the Old Latin Codex Vercellensis have "because God is a Spirit, and of God it is born."

John iii. 8 has, "*so are they which are born*

of water and the Spirit" (with Codex Sinaiticus, the Curetonian, and some Old Latin MSS.).

And John iii. 13, "*The Son of man, which is from heaven.*" This has no corroboration ; but it seems to be an improvement.

In John iii. 23 we have the name Ænon, explained as "Ain Nun," the Fish Spring.

In chap. iv. of St John's Gospel we have several very interesting variants. We have also a rearrangement of the narrative ; for ver. 7 comes between vers. 8 and 9.

In ver. 5 we read, "*a certain town of the Samaritans, which was called Shechem,*" instead of "Sychar." Some light is thrown upon this by a statement of St Jerome, quoted by Tischendorf. Under the name Sichar in *De nominibus Hebraicis*, he says : "Corrupte autem pro Sichem quae transfertur in humeros, ut Sichus legeretur usus obtinuit." And again, "Alioquin Hebraice Sichem dicitur : ut Joannes quoque evangelista testatur : licet vitiose ut Sichar legatur, error inolevit : et est nunc Neapolis urbs Samaritanorum" (*Quaest. Hebr.* in *Genesim*).

Ver. 6.—"*and the fountain of water of Jacob was there.*" Orientals make so decided a distinction between the *'ain*, "spring, fountain," πηγὴ, βρύσις, and the *bîr*, "well," φρέαρ, that we wonder to find both words used in the same narrative. A well is something that has been dug or formed artificially, whereas in the spring or fountain the water gushes naturally from the ground. What is now shown as Jacob's Well, near Nablûs, certainly is a well. Perhaps it might deserve both epithets, for it may have been fed from a fountain near at hand on Mount Gerizim.

Ver. 8 is here placed between vers. 6 and 7, and the fact that our Lord had sat down is twice repeated. "*And our Lord came and sat above the fountain . . . that He might rest from the toil of the way. And His disciples had gone up to that town to buy themselves food. And while our Lord sat, it was the sixth hour. And there cometh a certain woman of Samaria,*" etc. (with the Curetonian).

Ver. 23.—"*for the Father even seeketh these worshippers, those who worship Him in spirit and in truth.*" This is a repetition of the idea in the former clause of the verse (almost with Codex B of the Palestinian Syriac Version, and the Old Latin Codex Veronensis).

Ver. 25.—"*He will give everything.*"

Ver. 27.—"*And while they were talking, His disciples came and wondered that with the woman He was standing and talking.*"

This slight detail in the narrative is found, so far as we know, in no other manuscript. But it is quite in keeping with our Lord's character that He should have forgotten His own weariness, and should have risen to His feet in order to impress more vividly on the woman those great truths which He was revealing to her. And the change of attitude may have been prompted by an innate feeling of the chivalry which was eventually to blossom out of His teaching. Standing is not the usual habit of the Jewish Rabbi when he is engaged in teaching, so it is all the more remarkable that our Lord should have shown so much courtesy to our sex in the person of one of its most degraded representatives. The little word *qâem*, "standing," has so much significance, that we cannot suppose it to be a mere orthographical variant.

The word *qâem* is also found in the Armenian Commentary on the Diatessaron, translated into Latin by Moesinger. Before the discovery of the Sinai text, it was supposed to be merely what the French would call a "façon de parler," "a manner of speaking." Dr Burkitt has still an idea that it is so. He finds it elsewhere in this Gospel, in John vii. 26. The cases are, however, very different. When our Lord was addressing a great crowd in a public place, it was only natural that He should be "standing and speaking." Not so when He was tired and hungry in the hottest hour of the day.

Christian workers will be interested to know from John iv. 36 that "*And the reaper straightway*[1] *receiveth wages*" (with Codd. Bezæ, Veronensis, and the Curetonian).

In John v. 18 we are told, "*But the Jews sought to kill Him, because of this word, not only*

[1] Or "already."

because He had broken the sabbath, but because He had called God His Father, and He was comparing Himself with God."

In John v. 19 we are told that "*the Son can do nothing of Himself, which he doth not also see the Father do; and He doeth [nothing] except what the Father hath done. The Son also doeth likewise.*"

In John vi. 19 we read, "*And when they had brought it* (*i.e.* the ship) *about five stadia or thirty* (the word "twenty" must have dropped out, or be hidden below the upper script of the palimpsest), *and they saw Jesus, who came walking on the water, and He wished to pass by them; and when He drew near to their ship, they became pale with their fear.*"

And in John vi. 22, "*And the next day there was a crowd; and it saw that there was a certain boat in which His disciples had crossed; and our Lord Himself was not with them, and no other ship was beside them save the one into which the disciples had ascended.*"

In John vi. 47 we have, "*He that believeth on God hath life*" (almost with the Curetonian).

And in John vi. 51, "*And he who eateth of My bread shall live for ever.*"

Also in John vi. 63, "*It is the Spirit that quickeneth the body; but ye say, the body profiteth nothing.*"

In John vi. 68, 69, Simon Cephas says, "*Lord, to whom shall we go? Thou hast the word of eternal life. And we have believed and known that thou art the Christ, the Son of God*" (with several Old Latin MSS., almost with Codex Alexandrinus, the Curetonian, the Peshiṭta, and the Palestinian Syriac; the Curetonian omits "*the Christ,*" and the others add "*living*" before God). This emphasises the higher degree of knowledge possessed by Simon Peter over that of John the Baptist, as shown in John i. 34. It is observed in the majority of ancient manuscripts.

In John vii. 1 we are told that "*after these things Jesus walked in Galilee; because He would not walk openly in Judæa.*"

In John vii. 21 our Lord says, "*I have done one work in your sight, and ye all marvel*" (with the Curetonian).

In John vii. 45 we are told, "*And these officers returned, and came to those multitudes and to the Pharisees; and the priests and the Pharisees said unto them, Why have ye not brought Him?*"

And in John vii. 48, 49 that the Pharisees said, "*For who of the chief men or of the Pharisees has believed on Him? only this mob, who knoweth not the law.*" "Are accursed" is omitted.

In John vii. 53–viii. 11, *i.e.* the story of the woman taken in adultery, is omitted (with Codd. Sinaiticus, Vaticanus, and many other ancient Greek MSS.; also with some Old Latin MSS.). Tischendorf says that St John certainly never wrote this narrative, but that it is found in the MSS. of his Gospel from the third century onward. Dr Hort says that "the argument which has weighed most in its favour in modern times is its own internal character," but that "it presents serious differences from the diction of St John's Gospel, which strongly suggests diversity of authorship.

"When the whole evidence is taken into consideration," he continues, "it becomes clear that the section first came into St John's

Gospel as an insertion in a comparatively late Western text, having originally belonged to an extraneous independent source. That this source was either the *Gospel according to the Hebrews* or the *Expositions of the Lord's Oracles* of Papias is a conjecture only; but it is a conjecture of high probability.

"Erasmus showed by his language how little faith he had in its genuineness."

This section stands after Luke xxi. 38 in the archetype of the Ferrar group of Greek MSS., in what Dean Alford considers to be its apparent chronological place; though why it should have dropped out of Luke's Gospel cannot be readily explained.

With regard to this passage and two other interpolated ones, we must recollect that they all have the prestige of tradition in their favour; and that though they may never have been penned by the Evangelist in whose narrative they occur, they are records of what was believed by Christians of the Apostolic age, from whose memory the genuine words and deeds of the God-Man had not yet faded.

As such they are entitled to our profound respect, especially when they harmonise so well as this does with our Lord's life and character.

One might hazard a conjecture that Luke was the first to commit the narrative to writing, and that he did so after he had published both recensions of his Gospel. Perhaps it was added to St John's Gospel, for convenience sake, that the Church might become acquainted with it at an early period.

In John viii. 34 we read, "*Whoso committeth sin is a slave*"; "of sin" is omitted (with Codex Bezæ). The passage gains in force by this omission.

There is here a play on two Aramaic words, ʽabed "to do," and ʽabd, "a slave." This is supposed to be an indication that our Lord was speaking Aramaic, *i.e.* Syriac.

Ver. 56.—"*Abraham was longing to see My day*"; "Your father" being omitted (almost with the Peshiṭta).

Ver. 57.—"*The Jews say unto Him, Thou art not fifty years old and hath Abraham seen*

Thee?" (with the Codex Sinaiticus, and the uncorrected text of the Codex Vaticanus).

We owe the discovery of this corroboration to my friend the late Mr Theodore Harris, who was one of the Committee of the British and Foreign Bible Society. On seeking for this verse in the *facsimile* editions of the two oldest of Greek codices, he found that the Sinaiticus agrees perfectly with the reading of our palimpsest. Tischendorf has printed it *καὶ 'Αβραὰμ ἑώρακένσε*, etc., in his edition of 1865, and has noticed its existence in the critical notes to his Greek Testament. In the Codex Vaticanus the facsimile shows that a letter has been altered, and a space at the end of the sentence is blank, where perhaps the letter ε once existed. Thus ΚΑΙΑΒ̱ΡΑΑΜΕΟΡΑΚΕΣΕ has become ΚΑΙΑΒ̱ΡΑΑΜΕΟΡΑΚ$\overset{\text{Α}}{\hat{\text{Ε}}}$Σ. How necessary it is sometimes to seek light from the manuscripts themselves! This ancient though newly recovered reading is surely more appropriate to the narrative than the conventional one.

One cannot help thinking that our Lord

referred here to an incident in Abraham's life which has not been recorded in Holy Writ. May not a revelation about our Lord's day have been made to him by the angel on Mount Moriah, who had stayed his hand from slaying Isaac? Abraham was called the Friend of God. And surely real friendship demands sympathy. A father's sorrow in the prospect of losing his only son would prepare the patriarch for understanding the sacrifice which God even then was preparing to make for the salvation of the human race—that of the Lord Jesus, the Christ, on Calvary.

If this conjecture should be correct, God's proving of Abraham would have a deeper purpose than the trial of his faith, or the prohibition of human sacrifices.

John ix. 4 has, "*And I must work the works of Him that sent Me while it is day*," etc. (with our Authorised Version, Codex Alexandrinus, some Old Latin MSS., and the Peshiṭta).

John ix. 7 says, "*Go, wash thy face in the pool of Shiloah. And when he had washed his face, his eyes were opened*" (with the Coptic Version).

In John ix. 35 our Lord asks the man whom he had healed: "*Dost thou believe on the Son of man?*" Although it is recorded that our Lord tacitly assented when the title "Son of God" was given to Him by others, and bestowed a warm commendation on Simon Peter for using it towards Himself, we never elsewhere find the phrase in His own mouth, except through the malicious witness of His enemies. We therefore think that our palimpsest retains the true reading (with Codd. Sinaiticus, Vaticanus, and Bezæ).

It will be noticed that in this version of the blind man's story some of the repetitions which detract from the literary grace of the usual text are absent.

Two well-known German scholars, Dr Arnold Meyer and Dr Lietzmann, have tried to impress on us the idea, that "the Son of man" was no distinctive title, but merely a too literal rendering of the common Syriac word, "bar nasha," "a man." I have two cogent reasons for disagreeing with them:

(1) "The Son of man," *ὁ υἱὸς τοῦ ἀνθρώπου*,

as used by our Lord, is never translated into Syriac by "bar nasha"; but by the more emphatic and more stately "Breh de ansha."

(2) Those who translated our Lord's sayings into Greek must have seen something much more emphatic than "bar nasha," the common word for *ἄνθρωπος*, "man," in His designation of Himself. Why did they translate "bar nasha" by "the Son of Man"? and by "man" in the same chapter, nay, sometimes in the same verse? For instance, in Matt. xi. 19; xvi. 13; xvii. 22; xxvi. 24; Mark ii. 27, 28; ix. 31; xiv. 21; Luke vii. 34; ix. 44, 56; xii. 8; xxii. 22; xxiv. 7. If "bar nasha" is at the root of *ὁ υἱὸς τοῦ ἀνθρώπου*, what Syriac word is at the root of *ἄνθρωπος*?

The men who translated our Lord's sayings from Syriac into Greek, and those others who translated them back again into Syriac, must have been better acquainted with their own native tongue than even any German professor of the present day. Dr Wellhausen says very truly that he cannot believe that our Lord ever called Himself simply "the Man."

John x. 6 says, "*These things Jesus spake with them in a parable; and they did not understand.*" Here again the manuscript loses nothing by its conciseness.

In John x. 12 we have, "*But the false hireling, whose own the sheep are not.*"

In John x. 14 we have a repetition, "*I am the good shepherd, and know mine own, and mine own know Me; and I am known of mine, even as My Father knoweth Me, and I know My Father.*"

In John x. 16 the distinction between the several folds and the one flock is accurately reproduced in the Sinai MS.

In John xi. 18 we read how "*Bethany was distant from Jerusalem fifteen stadia, which are two miles.*"

And in John xi. 39, "*Martha saith unto Him, Lord, why are they lifting away the stone? Behold, he stinketh, because he hath been four days.*"

And in ver. 41, "*Then those men who were standing, came near, and raised the stone.*"

In ver. 43 we are told that Jesus cried with

a loud voice, "*Lazar, come forth, come out.*" It is well known that Lazarus is the Greek form of Eleazar. Most names are without the termination *ος* or "us," in Syriac.

In John xi. 48 the chief priests and Pharisees say, "*and the Romans will come, taking away our city and our nation.*" The mention of "our city," instead of "our place," seems very natural on the lips of those whose national hopes centred in Jerusalem.

In John xi. 57 we are told, "*And the chief priests and the Pharisees commanded that whosoever should see Him,*" etc., instead of "that if any man knew where He was."

In John xii. 2, 3, we find "*And he made Him a supper there; and Lazar was one of those seated at meat who were sitting with Him, but Martha was cumbered with service. Now Mary took an alabaster box of a pound of ointment of pure good spikenard of great price, and poured it on the head of Jesus while He sat at meat, and she anointed His feet, and wiped them with her hair,*" etc. The alabaster box is mentioned in the Peshiṭta. It may possibly have come from the narrative of a similar occurrence in the house of Simon the leper, as told in Luke vii. 37. But there is no reason why it should not belong to both incidents.

John xii. 12 begins, "*And on the next day He went out, and came to the Mount of Olives, and those great multitudes who had come to the feast,*" etc. This may be an interpolation from Luke xix. 29.

In John xii. 14 we have, "*as it is written by Zakaria the prophet, Fear not, daughter of Zion,*" etc. The name Zakaria is correct, though we have not seen it in any other MS.

In John xii. 29 we have, "*And the people that were standing there, and heard* [*it*], *wondered, and said that it had been thunder;*" etc.

John xii. 44 has, "*But Jesus cried out and said, He who is not like unto Me is not like unto Him that sent Me. And he who believeth in Me, believeth not in Me, but in Him that sent Me.*" We find a phrase something like this in one of Mar Ephraem's writings. "He who is like unto God," etc.[1]

[1] See Overbeck's Edition, p. 106, line 7.

And in John xii. 48, "*Whoso asketh Me, and receiveth not My words, there is one who judgeth him*," etc. This singular reading foretells the condemnation of those who deliberately reject our Lord's message.

In John xiii. 34, "that ye also love one another" is omitted. It is superfluous.

John xiv. 1 begins, "And then Jesus said, *Let not your heart be troubled: believe in God, and in Me ye are believing*." This clear assertion by our Lord of His own Divinity implies no change in the ordinary Greek text, for the first πιστεύετε may be either a present indicative or an imperative; and the second likewise. The Syriac, we are glad to say, is not dubious.

It is noteworthy that when, in 1895, I told the Sinai monks of this variant, as I called it, they at once replied, "That is the way we have always understood these words." Other members of the Greek Orthodox Church have said the same thing.

John xiv. 4 has, "*And whither I go ye know, and the way ye know*." This is the old reading of the Authorised Version (with Codd. Alexandrinus, Bezæ, and some Old Latin MSS., the Peshiṭta, and the Palestinian Syriac).

John xiv. 14 is omitted, with the Palestinian Syriac, some of the best Greek cursives, and the Old Latin Codex Veronensis. It is a repetition of ver. 13; which may have brought comfort to men of feeble faith. Our Lord's promises, however, do not require such confirmation.

In John xiv. 22, "*Thoma saith unto Him, Our Lord, how is it that Thou wilt manifest Thyself unto us,*" etc. The Curetonian has "*Juda Thoma*"; all other MSS. have "*Judas (not Iscariot).*"

Eusebius tells us that the real name of Thomas (the Twin) was Judas (*H.E.* i. 13).[1] Thirty-six pages of the Syriac *Acts of Judas Thomas* follow the text of the Four Gospels as the underscript in the Sinai Palimpsest (see *Horæ Semiticæ*, Appendix No. III.).

In John xv. 7, 8 our Lord says, "*But if ye*

[1] ἀπέστειλεν αὐτῷ Ἰούδας ὁ καὶ Θωμᾶς Θαδδαῖον ἀπόστολον, ἕνα τῶν ἑβδομήκοντα.

abide in Me, and My words in you, all that ye wish to ask shall happen unto you; because My Father will be glorified when ye yield much (fruit), and ye shall be My disciples."

And in John xv. 24, "*And if I had not done in their presence* (lit., *eyes*) *the works which none other man did, they had not had sins; but now they have seen My works, and have hated Me, and have hated My Father.*"

John xvi. 3, "And these things will they do unto you, because they have not known the Father nor Me," is omitted. So far as I know, the Sinai Palimpsest is the only extant MS. in which this verse is wanting.

In John xvi. 14, 15 we have an unusual punctuation. "*And it* (*the Spirit of truth*) *shall glorify Me, because it shall take of Mine, and shall declare it unto you; for what is the Father's is Mine: therefore said I unto you, that It shall take of Mine, and shall shew it unto you.*"

The word "Spirit" is feminine in Syriac, and is therefore rendered by the neuter in English. But it is not therefore impersonal; for the neuter gender of nouns does not exist in Syriac.

In John xvi. 16 our Lord says, "*and again a little while, and ye shall see Me, for I go unto My Father*" (with our Authorised Version).

In John xvi. 18, "We know not what He saith" is omitted.

In John xvi. 25, "I shall no more speak unto you in proverbs, but," is omitted. It is not quite necessary for the sense.

In vers. 25, 26, 27 we have, "*My Father,*" instead of "the Father." Only Codex Bezæ has "My Father," in ver. 26.

In John xvi. 27 we read, "*and have believed that I came out from God*" (with our Authorised Version).

In John xvi. 28, "I came out from the Father," and "I leave the world," are omitted. The first of these is only a repetition of the preceding clause. Ver. 28 therefore reads, "*I am come into the world, and again I go to the Father,*"—thirteen words as against twenty-two of the Revised Version. We do not think that the chapter loses anything in force by the absence of these repetitions ; on the contrary, it gains in literary beauty.

In John xvi. 30 the disciples say, "*Now we know that thou knowest all things, and needest not that thou shouldest ask any man ; by this we believe that thou art sent from God.*"

We have found no corroboration for this reading ; but it carries its own recommendation in itself : for it was surely a more natural thing for the disciples to say than, "and needest not that any man should ask Thee."

In John xvi. 31 we have, "*Jesus said unto them, Behold, now ye believe in Me.*"

In chap. xvii. of St John's Gospel the Sinai text omits some of the repetitions which are found in other MSS. I therefore think it will be agreeable to my readers to see it in full. The arrangement of punctuation by which the exclamation, "O my righteous Father!" is attached to the end of ver. 24, rather than to the beginning of ver. 25, is found also in Codex Bezæ. It may possibly be the same in Codex Sinaiticus, for there we find no punctuation to guide us.

"1 *And when Jesus had said these things, He
lifted up His eyes to heaven, and said, My Father,
the hour is come; glorify Thy Son, that Thy Son
may glorify Thee:* 2 *as Thou hast given Him
power over all flesh, that to every one whom Thou
hast given Him, He should give eternal life.*
3 *This is life eternal, that they should know Thee,
that Thou only art the God of truth, and Him
whom Thou hast sent, Jesus the Christ.* 4 *I have
glorified Thee on the earth: and the work which
Thou gavest Me to do I have finished.* 5 *And
now also give Me the glory, My Father, from
beside Thyself, from that which Thou gavest Me
when the world was not yet.* 6 *And I have
manifested Thy name unto the men whom Thou
gavest Me out of the world; for Thine they were,
and Thou gavest them Me; and they have kept
Thy word.* 7 *And now I have known that all
which thou hast given Me is from Thee:* 8 *because
the words which Thou hast given Me I have given
them; and they have received them from Me and
have known surely that I came out from Thee,
and they have believed that Thou didst send Me.*
9 *And I pray for their sake: and I pray not for*

the sake of the world, but for them which Thou
hast given Me; for they are Thine. 10 *And all*
that is Mine is Thine, and Thine is Mine: and I
am glorified in them. 11 *And henceforth I am not*
in the world, and these are in the world, and I
come to Thee. O My holy Father, take, keep them
in Thy name! 12 *While I was with them in the*
world, I kept them in Thy name: and not one of
them is lost, but the son of perdition; that what
is written might be fulfilled. 13 *Now I come to*
Thee; and these things I speak in the world, that
they may be filled with My joy. 14 *I have given*
them Thy word; and the world hateth them,
because they are not of it. 15 *I beseech Thee not*
that Thou shouldest take them out of the world, but
that Thou shouldest keep them from the evil;[1] 16 *for*
they are not of the world, even as I am not of it.
17 *Sanctify them by Thy truth: because Thy word*
is the truth. 18 *As Thou hast sent Me into the*
world, I also have sent them into the world.
19 *And for their sakes I sanctify Myself, that*
they also might be sanctified through the truth.
20 *Neither do I pray to Thee for the sake of these*

[1] Or, "the evil one."

alone, but also for the sake of those who shall
believe from their word; 21 *that they all may be*
one; even as Thou, My Father, art in Me, and I
in Thee, that they also may abide in Me, that the
world may believe that Thou hast sent Me. 22 *And*
the glory which Thou gavest Me I have given
them; that they may be one, even as we are one;
23 *I shall be with them, and Thou with Me; that*
they may become perfect in one; that the world may
know that Thou hast sent Me, and hast loved them,
even as, Father, Thou hast loved Me. 24 *And*
what Thou hast given Me, I will that where I am,
these may also be with Me; that they may behold
the glory which Thou hast given Me; and that
Thou hast loved Me before the world was, O my
righteous Father! 25 *And the world hath not*
known Thee: but I have known Thee, and those
have known that Thou hast sent Me. 26 *And I*
have made known unto them Thy name, and will
make it known: so that the love wherewith Thou
hast loved Me may be in them, and I also may be
in them."

It is sometimes said that the repetitions in the received text of this chapter are very valuable, because they emphasise the wonderful truths contained in it. We may be permitted to think, however, that it is a case of painting the lily ; and that the Sinai text gains in literary beauty by their absence.

CHAPTER IX

VARIANTS IN JOHN—*continued*

In John xviii. 1 we are told that Jesus went "*with His disciples over the brook of Kedron,* [*to*] *the mountain* [or *field*], *a place where there was a garden,*" etc. The traditional site of Gethsemane is at the beginning of the ascent of the Mount of Olives. The Syriac word "tûr" is sometimes translated "field," and means a place where the vegetation is wild, without any cultivation. If we take it in this sense, it would mean that Gethsemane was the only garden near the place.

John xviii. 3 tells us, "*But Judah, the betrayer, brought with him a band, and some of the chief priests and Pharisees, and officers, and a crowd of people carrying lanterns and lamps, and he came thither.*" "Weapons" are not mentioned.

John xviii. 12 says, "*and the chiliarch,*" instead of "the chief captain" (with Codd. Sinaiticus, Vaticanus, Alexandrinus, Bezæ, the Peshiṭta, and the Coptic).

After ver. 13 comes ver. 24, and this is one of the crowning excellences of this Antiochene codex. I had observed, when preparing my translation for the press in 1894 and 1896, that the arrangement of verses in this chapter was far superior to any that I had hitherto seen, because it gives us the story of our Lord's examination before Caiaphas, and then of Peter's denial, as two separate narratives, instead of being pieced into each other in the way with which we are familiar. The sequence is vers. 13, 24, 14, 15, 19, 20, 21, 22, 23, 16, 17, 18, 25, 26, 27, 28, 29, 30, 31. After this three leaves are unfortunately lost.

It was left to Dr Blass, of Halle, to discern and to say that the occurrence of ver. 24, that is, of the statement, "*But Hannan sent Him bound unto Caiapha the high priest,*" betwixt vers. 13 and 14, removes a discrepancy between the Gospel of St John and the

Synoptics; because it makes St John agree with the other Evangelists in stating that our Lord's trial took place in the house of Caiaphas instead of in that of Annas, as has been hitherto supposed. The attempt to explain away this apparent discrepancy gave rise to various ingenious hypotheses on the part of writers in the *Sunday School Chronicle* for May 14, 1899, when the International Lesson was taken from John xviii. 15–27.

It never occurred to any of them that a far simpler explanation had already been found, the displacement of ver. 24.

In editing the Palestinian Syriac Lectionary I have detected a slight corroboration of this in Codex A, the so-called *Evangeliarium Hierosolymitanum* of the Vatican Library (Lesson 150). Here ver. 24 occurs in two places: once after ver. 13, and once after ver. 23, as if the scribe had been uncertain as to its right location, or as if a tradition about its true place had been known to the original translators.

Dr Blass, in his *Philology of the Gospels*, p. 59, says about this section of chap. xviii. vers.

12–27 : "This is the narrative of a real author ; the other one is that of blundering scribes."

My powers of judgment on these difficult subjects are a very long way behind those of Dr Blass. I have neither the learning, the experience, nor the critical acumen which give so much weight to his opinions. So it is with the greatest diffidence that I would suggest the possible occurrence of similar phenomena in the seventeenth chapter of St John's Gospel, and in the narrative of the institution of the Lord's Supper, as given in Luke xxii. 14–23.

But, it may be asked, "How is it possible for such displacements to occur ?" Nothing, I regret to say, is simpler to the minds of those who have tried to read very ancient Greek manuscripts of the Bible. These are written in narrow columns, after the fashion of what was on the papyrus strips ; two, three, or even four columns being on each page. If a scribe, through inadvertence or interruption, happened to omit a phrase, he would write it in, either on the margin or in the space betwixt two of the columns, with a suitable mark in the text to indicate where it ought to be. Another man copied that page, perhaps two years, perhaps two centuries afterwards, and re-incorporated the marginal addition into the text. But he failed to understand his predecessor's reference mark; and so *he wrote it in the wrong column.* If this occurred in a very early copy, it would, of course, affect many subsequent ones.

The explanation of this difficulty was seen by Dr Martin Luther. In his edition of the German Bible, A.D. 1545, he says in a marginal note to ver. 14, "here ought to follow the verse 'And Hannes sent Him bound unto the high priest Caiphes,' *Infra* misplaced by the scribe in the turning of a leaf, what often happens." We wonder if Luther had heard of any MS. where the true sequence of these verses is followed; or if his keen intellect discerned it without any help from outside.

I shall, however, for convenience' sake, follow the usual text in my list of variants.

Vers. 24 and 14 are really one. "*But Hannan sent Him bound unto Caiapha the high priest, he which gave counsel to the Jews,*" etc.

Ver. 15.—"*But Simon Cepha and one of the disciples, he was known to the high priest, because of this he went with Jesus into the palace.*" A word seems to have been dropped out of this verse. Or perhaps it was only a single letter, and we ought to read "they went," instead of "he went."

John xviii. 17 tells us, "*When the handmaid of the door-keeper saw Simon, she said unto him,*" etc. It is reasonable, with our knowledge of Eastern customs, to believe that the door-keeper of the high priest's house was a man. While the daughter or the slave-girl of such a one might linger about the place, during the small hours of the night, properly veiled, and listen to the conversation of the men who were guarding their prisoner, it requires a considerable effort of imagination to conceive that the responsible duties of a porter or janitor were entrusted to a woman.

John xviii. 18 says, "*Now there were standing there servants and the officers, and they had laid for themselves a fire in the court to warm themselves; because it was freezing*" (with the

Peshiṭta). Jerusalem stands on very high ground, and at Easter time the nights there are often bitterly cold.

In John xviii. 19 we read, "*Now the high priest asked Jesus about His disciples, who they were, and about His doctrine, what it was.*"

And in John xviii. 22, "*When He had thus spoken, one of the officers which stood by struck Jesus on His cheek, and said unto Him*" (with the Peshiṭta, and almost with the Old Latin Codd. Vercellensis and Monacensis).

In John xviii. 23, "*Jesus said unto him, I have spoken well; why smitest thou Me?*"

In John xviii. 27, "*And again Simon denied, I know Him not,*" etc.

And in John xviii. 28, "*And when it dawned, they led Jesus from Caiapha, and brought Him to the hall of judgment, to deliver Him to the governor: but they went not into the judgment hall,*[1] *that they should not be defiled whilst they were eating the unleavened bread.*"

John xviii. 32–xix. 39 are on three lost leaves.

[1] Or "prætorium."

John xix. 42 tells us, "*And hastily, suddenly, they laid Him in the new sepulchre, which was nigh at hand, because the sabbath was dawning.*"

And John xx. 1, "*And at night, as the first day of the week was dawning, while it was yet dark in the early morning, came Mary the Magdalene to the sepulchre,*" etc. Here we are reminded that the uncouth expressions of the Greek and Latin manuscripts, Τῇ δὲ μιᾷ τῶν σαββάτων, and "una autem sabbati," are the literal rendering of a well-known Syriac idiom, *ḥad beshaba.* This has excited the suspicion that some Aramaic narrative, either written or oral, lies behind the Greek of St John's Gospel. And in this connection we may observe that the curious Greek of Rev. i. 8 is rendered by perfectly grammatical Syriac.

In John xx. 6, 7 we are told, "*But Simon, when he arrived, went in and saw the linen clothes, and the napkin that was rolled up together, and placed apart.*" This is more concise than the usual reading; but it is not so explicit.

And in John xx. 8, "*and they saw, and*

believed" (with B and C of the Palestinian Syriac Lectionary).

In this verse the phrase "which came first to the tomb" is omitted.

This is one of five slight touches, which all bring into prominence the fact that John's eagerness, and consequent success, was greater than Peter's. These touches are the words "other," "more quickly," and "first" in ver. 4; and "following him" in ver. 6, with "which came first to the tomb," in ver. 8. None of them appear in the Sinai text. Is it possible that the writer of this Gospel contented himself with stating the undoubted fact, that he, the beloved disciple, did outrun Simon, and came to the sepulchre? and then the first admiring copyist of his narrative introduced a few extra touches, to bring John's success into prominence? If this inference be correct, it is interesting to observe that he who once tried to secure a promise that he and his brother James should be first in their cousin's kingdom, became in his old age the modest disciple who forbore to append his own name to his Gospel. Is this not a delicate indication that the Apostle and the Evangelist were one and the same person? Peter, no doubt, was weighted by the recollection of his own sinful cowardice.

In John xx. 10 we read, "*But when the disciples saw these things, they went their way.*" The "ad se" of some Old Latin MSS., and the πρὸς ἑαυτοὺς, πρὸς αὐτοὺς, or πρὸς αὑτοὺς of the Greek text, seem to be a literal translation of a common Syriac idiom meaning simply "went away."

In John xx. 12 we are told of Mary Magdalene. "*And saw there two angels in white garments, sitting one at the pillows of the place in which Jesus had been lying, and one at the feet.*" The word which I have translated "pillows" is in the Peshiṭta also. It occurs only in the plural, and is used elsewhere chiefly for the Latin *cervical*, and for the "bolster" arranged by Michal (see 1 Sam. xix. 13, 16).

And in John xx. 16, "*And she understood Him, and answered, saying unto Him, Rabbuli.*[1] *And she ran towards Him that she might touch*

[1] *I.e.* "My Master."

Him." This latter interpolation is found also in the Ferrar group of Greek MSS., and in the Palestinian Syriac. It is more easy to imagine why it should be there, than why, once being there, it should have been omitted.

In John xx. 19, "When therefore it was evening" is omitted. Owing to the difference between our own computation and that of the Jews, we are sometimes at a loss as to the precise time of day at which an event took place. Presumably our Lord's appearance to His assembled disciples was before sunset, else it would have been on the second day of the week.

In John xx. 25 the disciples say, "*Our Lord is come, and we have seen Him.*"

In John xx. 26 we are told, "*And after eight days, on the next first* [*day*] *of the week.*"

In John xx. 27, "but believing" is omitted.

In John xxi. 6 we are told of the disciples, "*And when they had cast as He had said unto them, they sought to pull the net into the ship, and they could not for the weight of many fishes which it held.*"

And in John xxi. 7, of Simon, "*he took his coat, and girt it about his loins, and cast himself into the lake and was swimming, and came, for they were not far from the land.*"

In John xxi. 8, "for they were not far from the land, but about two hundred cubits off" is omitted, the first part of it being in ver. 7. "Full of fishes" is also omitted.

In John xxi. 9 we read that His disciples "*found before Jesus live coals of fire.*"

And in John xxi. 13, "*And Jesus took the bread and the fish, and blessed them* (lit., *blessed upon them*), *and gave unto them.*" The same expressions are used in Matt. xxvi. 26.

It cannot therefore have been anything peculiar to the bread and wine of the Lord's Supper.

John xxi. 15–18 has a very interesting arrangement, "*And when they had eaten, Jesus saith unto Simon, Thou* (*art*) *Simon, son of Jona, lovest thou Me? He saith unto Him, Yea, Lord. He saith unto him, Feed My lambs. Again Jesus saith unto him, Thou Simon, son of Jona, lovest thou Me much? He saith unto Him, Yea,*

Lord. He saith unto him, Feed My sheep. Again Jesus saith unto him, Simon, son of Jona, lovest thou Me? Simon was grieved because three times Jesus spake thus unto him. Simon said unto Him, Thou knowest all things; thou knowest that I love Thee? And He said unto him, Feed My flock."

"More than these" is omitted altogether. "Thou knowest that I love Thee" is omitted in ver. 15. "Much" occurs only in our Lord's second query; and "Thou knowest that I love Thee" only in Simon's third answer. There is therefore a gradation of intensity in the replies of both Simon and our Lord.

Another note of intensity comes into the prophecy about Peter in John xxi. 18, "*and shall drive thee whither thou wouldest not.*"

And into John xxi. 22, "*Follow Thou Me now.*"

In John xxi. 23, "what is that to thee?" is omitted (with Codex Sinaiticus, the Old Latin Codex Vercellensis, and the oldest form of the Palestinian Syriac Lectionary).

In John xxi. 25 we read, "*And Jesus did many other things, which if they were written one by one, the world would not suffice for them,"*—twenty-one words as against thirty-five of the Revised Version.

"*Here endeth the Gospel of the Mepharreshe four books. Glory to God and to His Christ, and to His Holy Spirit. Let everyone who reads and hears and keeps and does* [*it*] *pray for the sinner who wrote* [*it*]. *May God in His tender mercy forgive him his sins in both worlds. Amen and Amen.*"

The word *Mepharreshe* is a link between those two specimens of the Old Syriac version, the Syro-Antiochene Palimpsest and the Curetonian. In the latter it is prefixed to the Gospel of St Matthew alone; here it is evidently applied to all four. The word may be rendered either as "separate" or as "translated." The first meaning is in this case the more likely one, seeing that Tatian's Diatessaron was entitled the Meḥalleṭte, or "mixed." This, however, in no way affects our estimate concerning the age of the text, for the epithet might well be added by a fourth-century copyist.

Another peculiarity of the Sinai text is the

use of the word "*Maran*," "our Lord," instead of "Jesus," in a large portion of it. It occurs from Matt viii. 3 to xi. 7 and from John i. 38 to vi. 5.

This is supposed to be due to the reverent affection for the Saviour entertained by the translator.

Since I deciphered the dim lines which contain the first half of the final colophon (belonging to the upper script), from my photographs, on Good Friday 1900—lines containing the names of the district and of the monastery where this text of the Gospels was covered over in the eighth century with the "Select Narratives of Holy Women" (the district Antioch, the monastery Beth Mari-Qanūn), and since Mr Burkitt added thereto the name of the village Ma'arrath Meṣrin, from the late Professor Bensly's copy of a previous very clear colophon, every probability that this ancient text was produced at Mount Sinai has for ever vanished. True, it may have been brought to an Antiochene monastery from Egypt, from Mesopotamia, or from elsewhere, but old vellum was not likely to be a profitable export from the Arabian Desert ; and it would be passing strange if the finished palimpsest was really returned to the very monastery whence its half-written pages had been carried at some period before the eighth century. No, the earliest of Syriac versions was likely to be copied only where there was a native Syrian Church, and a seat of Syriac learning, such us was found at Antioch on the Orontes, or at Edessa. Rabbula, Bishop of Edessa, in the fifth century, issued a decree that a copy of the Separate Gospels should be read in every church instead of Tatian's Diatessaron. This copy was probably the Peshiṭta, perhaps as revised by himself,[1] for had it been the Old Syriac, surely more than two specimens of it would come down to the present day. The multiplication of copies of the Peshiṭta probably caused those of the Old Syriac to become obsolete, and fit only for the use of men like John the Stylite. The Diatessaron was perhaps

[1] See Dr William Wright on "Syriac Literature," in the *Encyclopædia Britannica*, Tenth Edition, p. 825.

written at Edessa, and there the Peshiṭta was revised. Now the Tales of Holy Women, which overlie the Gospels of our palimpsest, were certainly written near Antioch, and the last of them, Cyprian and Justa, has a distinctly Antiochene flavour, for there (as a reviewer in the *Scotsman* lately observed) its demon boasts of having "shaken the whole city, and overturned walls," alluding, doubtless, to the terrible earthquakes with which Antioch was visited in the first two centuries of our era. I may perhaps be mistaken, but I do not find it difficult to imagine that as the Peshiṭta was highly appreciated in Edessa, so the Old Syriac Version may have been cherished in the older seat of Aramaic learning, in the town where the disciples were first called Christians.

To sum up, we have seen that several important narratives, such as Luke xxii., John xvii., and John xviii. are better arranged and more concise than they are in any other text extant ; that several variants, such as those in Matt. xviii. 17 ; Mark xvi. 3 ; Luke i. 63, 64, vii. 29 ; John viii. 57, xvi. 30, xviii. 13–25, whether corroborated or not by other ancient manuscripts, bear within themselves a witness to their own truthfulness; that the chief agreement is with the so-called Western texts; but there are many variants which belong only to the palimpsest. These, however, bring into stronger relief the immense majority of passages in which its text is in close agreement with that of our Revised Version.

Tischendorf has pointed out that variants and even corruptions of the text are in themselves a strong proof that the Gospels were written in the first century; because there is not one of these which cannot be traced back to the second century; and the pure text is naturally older than its corruptions. The great aim of textual critics in the present day is to ascertain what that pure text is.

A still more difficult question presents itself. Why has God not protected the transmission of these sacred books? Why has He allowed variants to exist? The answer may be that His work is not mechanical, like ours. And is it not possible that we have ourself confounded the idea of inspiration with that of dictation?

The latter would have meant the production of a text whose every letter might have been worshipped ; the former means that God put into the hearts of chosen men the desire to write what they knew for a certainty about His dealings with them, but that He left them at perfect liberty both to express and to transmit His meaning in their own way.

CHAPTER X

A FEW SUGGESTED EMENDATIONS IN THE REVISED VERSION

After all the amount of skill, learning, and labour which have been expended with the object of giving us a perfect translation of the English Bible, a few captious people still exist who find some passages not sufficiently clear for their understandings. I am one of their number. I do not go so far as an old Congregationalist minister whom one of my friends had the advantage of hearing on a Sunday morning, a devout man whose sermon was really edifying to an attached flock, although it ended with the statement, "My brethren, I could have got a great deal more instruction out of that verse if the inspired writer had not put a comma into it." The good man was evidently not aware that the comma belonged to the translation ; for there is no punctuation in the ancient Greek manuscripts, nor even any division of the letters into words.

1 *Kings xvii*

The Old Testament Revisers have done splendid work, but they have not always had the courage of their opinions. Why, for instance, should they have persisted in telling us, twice over, that Elijah lay down under a juniper-tree, though every traveller who rides through the Sinai desert soon learns that the common, white-flowered broom-bush is called a "ratamah," almost the word which is used in 1 Kings xix. 4, 5, in Job xxx. 4, and in Ps. cxx. 4. The diffusion of knowledge is so great among the general public in our day (for the newspapers help it), that even the most learned of men would do well if he were to refrain from mystifying us, and from covering up the mistakes of his predecessors, by putting the right word with an "or" before it into the margin. Only in Job have they put "broom" into the text.

And it is very hard for me to believe that the juniper-bush, which I have seen growing in the dripping forests of Scotland, could also have a home in the almost waterless desert of Sinai. Robinson's authority is frequently quoted for this ; but when he speaks of the juniper, he evidently means the *rethem*. Major H. S. Palmer also had his scientific instincts perverted by his recollection of the Authorised Version, for he speaks of "the *retem* or broom, identical with the juniper of Scripture."

The botanical name of the juniper is given by both Badger and Wahrmund as *'ar'ar* the mountain-cypress. Badger gives also the names *Abhal* and "*kûklân*," which perhaps he took down from the lips of the Arabs. I am puzzled to know how a plant can both belong to the genus *cytisus* and the genus *coniferæ*.

Genesis xxxvii. 3

I am inclined also to protest against Joseph's coat being called a coat of many colours in the text, and "a long garment with sleeves" in the margin. If the colours are right, there is no need to think of it as patchwork; for many an Eastern maiden wears an apron which vies with the rainbow not so much in multiplicity of colours, as in the gradual blending of a few bright hues together. But if the word mean "sleeves," that ought to be in the text; and it is certainly a word whose significance is enhanced by the habits of the modern Bedawîn, whose sleeveless *abbayas* are easily slipped on and off, serving by turns the purposes of overcoat and of blanket.

1 *Kings xvii.* 6

"*And the ravens brought him (Elijah) bread and flesh in the morning, and bread and flesh in the evening; and he drank of the brook.*" Elijah seems to be unique among the prophets of Israel in having the minor details of his life misunderstood. To find a juniper-bush in the desert would, we imagine, be a greater miracle than to be fed by ravens; and yet the ravens also are now justly suspected to be there in mistake for the Bedawîn Arabs. The word "arab," in Hebrew, may mean the west, the sunset, a pledge, a crow, or a native of Arabia; and we know that the sons of the desert are not only famous for their hospitality to lonely, peaceful strangers, but they are to-day, as always, imbued with a profound respect for any person or thing that is in intimate relation with the unseen world. For instance, the Bedawîn of the Sinai peninsula firmly believe that the two tables of stone, on which Moses wrote the Ten Words, were built into the wall beneath the apse of the church in the Sinai Monastery, and this idea has done real service in preserving the convent from attack and pillage. What more natural, then, that out of the recorded fact, that Arabs brought food to Elijah, the Israelites should have read the word "Arabs" as "ravens," and that the earliest translators of Holy Writ, the LXX, from national vanity, should have adopted the dubious reading. We do not say that the ravens could not have acted thus; and we think that carrying flesh would have been more natural to them than carrying bread; but we need not resort to the idea of a miracle when there is a much more obvious translation ready to our hand. Why should we not have "or Arabs" in the margin?

1 *Kings xix.* 5

Even the angel, who told Elijah that a cake was lying baken on the coals, was doing what a Bedawy does every day of his life; only the coals were probably embers of the charcoal which is made in considerable quantities from the sapless little plants of the desert. And God sometimes makes use of mortal man to do the work of angels. The word which we translate "angel," in Hebrew as in Greek, has "messenger" for its primary meaning.

Romans i. 5, 6

Authorised Version.—"*By whom* (i.e. *Jesus Christ*) *we have received grace and apostleship, for obedience to the faith among all nations, by His name: among whom are ye also the called of Jesus Christ.*"

Revised Version.—"*Through whom we received grace and apostleship, unto obedience of faith among all the nations, for His name's sake: among whom are ye also, called to be Jesus Christ's.*"

It is in ver. 6 that I wish to point out the possibility of a misunderstanding. If the verse be read in solitude with one's eyes on the printed page, it may be all right. But the case is very different when it is read aloud in church. Once upon a time this came forcibly before my mind as I listened to the morning lesson. It was no fault of the reader. His tones were clear enough, but he could not make any distinction of sound between the nominative plural and the possessive singular; and for a few moments I thought that the New Testament actually contained a distinct warrant for a heresy which the British public (perhaps mistakenly) thought had been propounded a few years ago by the Rev. R. J. Campbell, of the City Temple; and which was enthusiastically upheld by a young Buddhist undergraduate in Cambridge, viz. that the difference between ourselves and the Incarnate Son of God is a difference in degree only; and that we may become His equals—not merely His humble servants and imitators. As well might the moon grow into a little sun, and cease to shine by reflected light! A glance at my Greek Testament relieved my mind, for I at once saw where the ambiguity lies. Our English language is clear and forcible, but as it lacks the grammatical niceties of Greek and Latin, some care ought surely to have been exercised to avoid a possible misunderstanding.

1 *Corinthians x.* 20

There are a number of instances in the New Testament where the Greek word *δαίμων*, "demon," is incorrectly translated "devil." We can excuse this in the Authorised Version, for the English scholars of King James's day were not sufficiently acquainted with the old Greek religion to appreciate what was meant by a "demon." Even in Milton's time we suspect that this was not understood, for the impression which we get from his description of the denizens of Hell leads us to attribute a greater degree of cruel malignity to demons than to devils. This idea has, in fact, set its stamp on our language; but it places the Greek demon in a false light, and makes us lose sight of the true meaning of St Paul's argument. The Greek demons were the inferior gods, intermediaries between Zeus and his creatures. Their true successors are the saints of the Roman Calendar. To them worship and sacrifice were quite naturally offered ; and to eat the flesh of animals that had been slain in their honour was in no sense to partake of a "table of devils," or malignant spirits. St Paul tells his correspondents that although these demons are imaginary beings, which have never had any real existence, and although it cannot do a Christian the slightest harm to partake of such food, if his faith be strong enough to realise this, yet, for the sake of those who cannot get rid of the spell of their fancied existence, circumstances may occur in which it would be wise for a Christian to refuse the consecrated viands. Men were never so wicked, even in heathen times, as to have a "table of devils." These, to the Jews, were very real beings ; and the whole cogency of St Paul's argument disappears if we are led to think that he is speaking of them.

Would it not then be wise to replace the word "demon" in the text of our English Bible wherever it appears in the margin and leave to old Satan only what is his own? such as the warning against him in Eph. iv. 27, "Neither give place to the Devil." We should then be on surer ground when we discuss the question of what is often called "demoniac possession." It is indeed passing strange that while the word "demon" is only once used in the Gospels, in the story of the Gadarene swine, (Matt. viii. 31), a diminutive form of it, "demonion," *pl.* "demonia," is frequently applied to the wicked spirits whom our Lord cast out. It is evident that the Jews had adopted this word; but I am convinced that St Paul used the word "demon" in its true sense.

Ephesians vi. 5

It is also open to question if the word δοῦλος should not be translated "slave." For free servants, who work for wages, the word ὑπηρέτης is invariably used in the New Testament; and the two sets of people are .ound standing together in John xviii. 18, where "the slaves and the servants" are incorrectly translated as "the servants and the officers." Another word for "servant," θεράπων, is applied to Moses in Heb. iii. 5. Surely the argument is greatly weakened by the substitution of "servant" for "slave."

We should lose nothing by this restitution, for St Paul's exhortations to slaves, with the possible exception of the "fear and trembling," are surely doubly incumbent on wage-earners, who receive a just equivalent for their work. We should bring into clearer relief the gentle manner in which Christianity gradually abolished slavery ; not by upsetting society through proclaiming the Rights of Man, and thus inciting the slaves to revolt ; but by putting just and humane principles into the minds of their masters. From the time of St Paul to that of Wilberforce, Clarkson, and Sturge is indeed a "far cry" ; but the slavery of white people disappeared in Europe at an early period. It began to do so in the second century. The heathen Africans were held in bondage much longer ; partly because they themselves had the minds of slaves, and partly because white men were wont to look on them more as cattle than as human beings. The slang expression "black-birding" for shooting savages shows that this idea has not wholly disappeared in our own day.

Philippians iii. 2

"*Beware of the dogs.*"

Revelation xxii. 15

"*Without are the dogs.*"

It is difficult to believe that St Paul interrupted his flow of profitable exhortation, and St John his description of the glories of heaven, to express their dislike for a generally harmless domestic animal which, even in their day, had, by its virtues, won its way into the affections of the human race. Accordingly most commentators think that they referred to some species of men ; to Judaisers, perhaps, or to people who, by their vices, had sunk even lower than the brutes. Perhaps we shall not go very far wrong if we suppose that cynics are meant, those snarling critics who never see any good in the character or work of their fellow-men, and to whom the old Greeks gave the name of κυνικοὶ, or dog-like. As many people never read a commentary on the Scriptures, I am sure that there are some so destitute of imagination as to think that real dogs are meant; and therefore I would venture to suggest that the words, "perhaps cynics," might be placed in the margin, and thus the quality of consistency would be restored to both these passages. Cynics would indeed be out of place in the New Jerusalem.

Hebrews vii. 18, 19

Authorised Version.—"*For there is verily a disannulling of the commandment going before for the weakness and unprofitableness thereof. For the law made nothing perfect, but the bringing in of a better hope did; by the which we draw nigh unto God.*"

Revised Version.—"*For there is a disannulling of a foregoing commandment because of its weakness and unprofitableness* (*for the law made nothing perfect), and a bringing in thereupon of a better hope, through which we draw nigh unto God.*"

Both these renderings are somewhat difficult to follow. My objection to that of the Authorised Version is, that I cannot see its truth. The bringing in of a better hope did not make anything perfect, for a hope is by its nature an incomplete thing. The Revisers have tried to overcome the difficulty by reading "for the law made nothing perfect" as a parenthesis; and thus attaching "and the bringing in of a better hope" to the "disannulling of a foregoing commandment." This is an improvement, but is the difficulty not capable of a simpler solution?

The central clause of ver. 19, "but the bringing in of a better hope," is expressed in Greek by four words, none of which is a verb. Few languages allow of such ellipses; you cannot put it into intelligible English without supplying a verb. Now I submit that the verb which most frequently needs to be supplied in these cases is the verb "to be"; and that we ought to try some tense of that simplest of all forms of expression before we resort to any other device. So may we not read: "*For the law made nothing perfect, but it was the bringing in of a better hope*"?

This is not only simpler, but it is the statement of an actual fact. The Law, not in the sense of the Ten Words, but in the sense of the Torah, with its sacrificial symbolism and its prophecies, did bring into the world a hope of deliverance from sin through the coming of a Redeemer. The whole Epistle to the Hebrews is a setting forth of this fact.

CHAPTER XI

SOME AGREEMENTS OF SCIENCE WITH BIBLE TEACHING

The Book of Nature is written by the finger of God, quite as much as the Bible is. Or perhaps it would be more correct to say, that the impress of God's finger is on every natural object on the face of our planet; and it is not difficult to find it, excepting only where it has been overlaid or obliterated by the clumsy art of man. The sign-manual of God is Beauty, both of form and of colour; beauty which it passes the wit of man to imitate, or even fully to appreciate.

This being so, if these two books are supposed in some cases to disagree, it must be because one of them has not been rightly read. I do not propose to try and explain alleged differences. That task would be beyond my powers, and also beyond the scope of this little work. But I think that there are some striking agreements, which often escape our notice, although they cannot well be explained—having regard to the ignorance of natural science which prevailed during the time when the thirty-nine books of the Old Testament and the twenty-six of the New Testament were written—except on the theory that the authors of these were divinely inspired. I content myself with placing the two teachings side by side. My readers may supply the comments.

Exodus i. 12

"*And they built for Pharaoh store-cities, Pithom and Raamses.*" Dr Edouard Naville has identified Pithom with Tell-el-Maskhutah, twelve miles from Ismailiah. It was wrongly named "Raamses" by M. Lepsius and the French engineers of the Suez Canal. Many of the monuments excavated by them are dedicated to the god "Tum." "Pi Tum" means "the abode of Tum." Amongst the broken statues found there is one of a squatting man in red granite, who is called "the good Recorder of Pi-tum"; also a fragment from the statue of a priest, on which M. Naville first read the name of the city, Pi-tum.

The city changed its name under a Greek dynasty, and became Heroopolis. M. Naville found within its walls chambers which appear to have been built for no other purpose than that of storehouses or granaries.—*The Store City of Pithom*, by Edouard Naville, Egypt Exploration Fund, 1885.

Exodus xx. 4–6

"*Thou shalt not make unto thee a graven image, nor the likeness of any form that is in heaven above, or that is in the earth beneath, or that is in the water under the earth: thou shalt not bow down thyself unto them nor serve them: for I the Lord thy God, am a jealous God, visiting the iniquity of the fathers upon the children, upon the third and upon the fourth generation of them that hate Me.*"

Also Ex. xxxiv. 7; Num. xiv. 18; Deut. v. 9.

Leviticus xxvi. 39

"*And they that are left oj you shall pine away in their iniquity in your enemies' lands; and also in the iniquities of their fathers shall they pine away with them.*"

"A woman who was sober becomes a drunkard. Her children born during the period of her sobriety are said to be quite healthy; her subsequent children are said to be neurotic. The quality of the mother's milk would be bad. The surroundings of the home under the charge of a drunken woman would be prejudicial to the health of a growing child. No wonder that it became neurotic!"—Francis Galton, *Natural Inheritance*, p. 15.

"Let us suppose a class of persons, called A, who are affected with some form and some specific degree of degeneracy . . . and let class B consist of the offspring of A. We already know only too well that when the grade of A is very low, that of the average B will be below par and mischievous to the community; but how mischievous will it probably be?"—

F. Galton, *Probability the Foundation of Eugenics*, p. 13.

"It is better that many guilty should escape, than that one innocent person should suffer. But that is not the sentiment by which natural selection is guided."—*Ibid.*, p. 14.

1 *Samuel v.* 1, 2, 6–12 ; *vi.* 1–2, 5, 12, 19

"*Now the Philistines had taken the ark of God, and they brought it from Eben-ezer unto Ashdod. And the Philistines took the ark of God, and brought it into the house of Dagon. . . . But the hand of the Lord was heavy upon them of Ashdod, and He destroyed them, and smote them with tumours, even Ashdod and the borders thereof. And when the men of Ashdod saw that it was so, they said, The ark of the God of Israel shall not abide with us: for His hand is sore upon us, and upon Dagon our Goa. They sent therefore and gatherea all the lords of the Philistines unto them, and said, What shall we do with the ark of the God of Israel? And they answered, Let the ark of the God of Israel be carried about unto Gath. And they carried the ark of the God of Israel about thither. And it was*

so, that, after they had carried it about, the hand of
the Lord was against the city with a very great
discomfiture : and He smote the men of the city, both
small and great, and tumours brake out upon them.
So they sent the ark of God to Ekron. And it came
to pass, as the ark of God came to Ekron, that the
Ekronites cried out, saying, They have brought about
the ark of the God of Israel to us, to slay us and our
people. They sent therefore and gathered together
all the lords of the Philistines, and they said, Send
away the ark of the God of Israel, and let it go again
to its own place, that it slay us not, and our people :
for there was a deadly discomfiture throughout all
the city ; the hand of God was very heavy there.
And the men that died not were smitten with the
tumours : and the cry of the city went up to heaven.
vi. *And the ark of the Lord was in the country of*
the Philistines seven months. And the Philistines
called for the priests and the diviners, saying,
What shall we do with the ark of the Lord ? . . .
Wherefore ye shall make images of your tumours,
and images of your mice that mar the land ; and ye
shall give glory unto the God of Israel : peradven-
ture He will lighten His hand from off you, and

from off your gods, and from off your land. . . . And the kine took the straight way by the way to Beth-shemesh; they went along the high way, lowing as they went, and turned not aside to the right hand or to the left; ana the lords of the Philistines went after them unto the border of Beth-shemesh. . . . And He (the Lord) smote of the men of Beth-shemesh, because they had looked into the ark of the Lord, even He smote of the people seventy men and fifty thousand men: and the people mourned, because the Lord had smitten the people with a great slaughter."

My sister, Mrs Gibson, reminds me that Sir Richard H. Charles pointed out a few years ago that while the ark was in the temple of Dagon, at Ashdod, the said temple was probably filled, night and day, with worshipers who would eat their meals in it, just as their successors do in the Church of the Holy Sepulchre in Jerusalem at the present day. Crumbs of food bring mice, mice bring fleas, fleas would find a pleasant lodging in the covering of badgers' skins wherewith the ark was covered (see Num. iv. 6). What wonder that the plague broke out in Ashdod and in every city to which the ark was carried! Its coverings were perhaps aired and cleaned by the men of Kiriath-jearim. A similar story happens, we may surmise, at the present day, both at Mecca and in India. Fleas carried by mice and rats are the most active propagators of bubonic plague. This cannot be called a proof of the authenticity of the first book of Samuel, but it may claim to be an interesting coincidence. Of the same nature is another narrative the explanation of which my sister remembers being suggested in a recent letter to the *Times*.

2 *Kings v.* 21–27

"*So Gehazi followed after Naaman. And when Naaman saw one running after him, he lighted down from the chariot to meet him, and said, Is all well? And he said, All is well. My master hath sent me, saying, Behold, even now there be come to me from the hill country of Ephraim two young men of the sons of the prophets; give them, I pray thee, a talent of silver, and two changes of raiment. And Naaman said, Be content, take two talents. And he urged him, and bound two talents of silver in two bags, with two changes of raiment, and laid them upon two of his servants, and they bare them before him. And when he came to the hill, he took them from their hand and bestowed them in the house: and he let the men go, and they departed. But he went in and stood before his master. And Elisha said unto him, Whence comest thou, Gehazi? And he said, Thy servant went no whither. And he said unto him, Went not mine heart with thee, when the man turned again from his chariot to meet thee? Is it a time to receive money, and to receive garments, and olive-yards and vine-yards, and sheep and oxen, and men-servants and maid-servants? The leprosy therefore of Naaman shall cleave unto thee, and unto thy seed for ever. And he went out from his presence a leper as white as snow.*"

Naaman had been miraculously cleansed by dipping seven times in the river Jordan. But the two changes of raiment which he gave to the greedy Gehazi (who so greatly resembled many an Oriental servant of the present day) had not been disinfected. Natural causes assisted in the traitor's punishment; as they did in the case of Herod Agrippa I. (Acts xii. 23), and in that of many another self-indulgent person.

The harsh sentence on Gehazi's seed is, it may be remarked, quite in accordance with the teachings of modern science in regard to some forms of leprosy.

Before we leave the subject of pestilence, we must refer to the terrible occurrence recorded in 2 Kings xix. 35, during the siege of Jerusalem by the Assyrians.

2 *Kings xix.* 35, 36

"*And it came to pass that night, that the angel of the Lord went forth, and smote in the camp of the Assyrians an hundred fourscore and five thousand: and when men arose early in the morning, behold, they were all dead corpses. So Sennacherib king of Assyria departed, and went and returned, and dwelt at Nineveh.*"

In the lately recovered Hebrew text of Sirach (Ecclesiasticus) we have the statement, xlviii. 21:

> "And He smote the army of Assyria
> And discomfited them with the plague."

With this agrees

2 *Kings xx.* 1, 7

"*In those days was Hezekiah sick unto death. . . . And Isaiah said, Take a cake of figs. And they took and laid it on the boil, and he recovered.*"

Hezekiah's sickness was evidently a case of bubonic plague.

In Herodotus (*Euterpe*, ii. 141) we find the statement that the army of "Sanacharib, king of the Arabians" (some MSS. add, "and of the Assyrians,") "encamped at Pelusium, was attacked at night by field mice, who ate the quivers, the bows, and the handles of the shields, so that they fled, and many perished." Could either Sirach or Herodotus have foreseen that these statements would be reconciled to each other by that modern science which has only lately discovered that the infection of plague is carried by rats?

Numbers xxxiii. 1–36

These verses contain a list of the stations where the children of Israel rested during their desert journey from Egypt to Sinai, and from Sinai to Kadesh, probably by way of 'Aqaba, which has been the trade-path between Egypt and Canaan from time immemorial. These stations coincide remarkably with the directions to modern travellers given in Murray's Guide-book to Egypt; [1] not in the place-names, it is true, but in the number of days required for all sections of the journey. And this goes far to confirm the claim of the traditional Sinai to be the Mount of the Law, and to destroy that put forward by Dr Charles Beke and others on behalf of a mountain named Djebel-en-Nur, on the eastern side of the Gulf of 'Aqaba, or of another as yet unidentified, in or near the Land of Edom. Taking Pi-ha-hiroth as the last station where the Israelites rested on Egyptian soil after they had crossed the Red Sea, we find that they encamped nine times before they reached the foot of Mount Sinai. Modern travellers do precisely the same; and their camels carry them, by wading, through a little bit of the sea on the afternoon of the

[1] This fact was observed by a member of the Survey Expedition.

fourth day after leaving Suez (Num. xxxiii. 10). After quitting the splendid plain of Er-Rahah, at the foot of the steep Râs-es-Sufsafah, the lowest of the three peaks of Sinai, where all the conditions described in the book of the Exodus are admirably fulfilled, they go to 'Aqaba, and on to Kadesh and Petra, in about seventeen days. The heavily-weighted Israelites encamped twenty times on this path ; but time was doubtless less of an object with them than it is with us.

I allow that few of the place-names in Num. xxxiii. can now be identified, but hills of pure sand, or even of bare rock, in the monotonous desert are seldom distinguished by any appellation ; therefore every tourist is free to call them what he will—either "Storm-hill," where the wind drove the sand unmercifully into his eyes, or "Ma idri," "I don't know," which was the response of his camel-driver to one of his queries. I suggest that most of these names may be derived from some incident which happened to the Israelites at each particular resting-place ; and as these were not made known to the Bedawîn of that day, they were naturally not perpetuated.

Dr Beke despised the traditional site so much that he never visited it, and to vindicate his conjecture he had to imagine another Mitzraim (Egypt) among the hills of soft sand about El Arish, only five days' journey from Canaan, and another Nile on its generally dry river-bed. Lastly, he had to confess that Djebel-en-Nur, like Djebel Musa, has never been a volcano, thus cutting away the root of his own prejudice against the latter. Any further attempts to diminish the fame of the traditional site are almost certain to end in a like failure, for the compiler of Num. xxxiii. has almost measured the distance between the frontier of Egypt and the sublime ramparts of granite which surround Er-Rahah, the plain of the Israelite "Rest."

1 *Kings xix.* 11, 12

"*And behold, the Lord passed by, and a great and strong wind rent the mountains, and brake in pieces the rocks before the Lord; but the Lord was not in the wind: and after the wind an earthquake; but the Lord was not in the earthquake; and after the earthquake a fire; but the Lord was not in the fire; and after the fire a still small voice.*"

Not alone at Sinai, but at St Pierre in 1902, at San Francisco and Valparaiso in 1906, and at Messina in 1908, did a wind precede an earthquake, and a fire follow it.

Psalm cxii. 1, 2

"*Blessed is the man that feareth the Lord, that delighteth greatly in His commandments. His seed shall be mighty upon earth: the generation of the upright shall be blessed.*"

"Among the successful graduates of Oxford and Cambridge, and among purely literary men, we find a much larger proportion of sons of clergymen."—F. Galton, *English Men of Science*, p. 23.

"*Thy law is the truth.*"—Ps. cxix. 142.

"*I am the Way, the Truth, and the Life.*"—John xiv. 6. *Cf.* Jer. x. 10.

"A hunger for truth is a frequent ingredient in the disposition of the abler men of every career."—F. Galton, *English Men of Science*, pp. 22, 23.

"A pious disposition is decidedly hereditary." —F. Galton, *Hereditary Genius*, p. 274.

"The children of very religious parents sometimes turn out extremely badly. It is a fact that has all the appearance of being a serious violation of the law of heredity."—*Ibid.*, p. 276.

In the life of Fidelia Fiske, the devoted Persian missionary, we have an instance of the covenant blessing descending not only through generations, but also through centuries. We read in her memoir:

"In the year 1637, two brothers, William and the Rev. John Fiske, emigrated from the county of Suffolk to America, settling first in Salem, Massachusetts. . . . They were children of pious and worthy parents, yea, of grand-parents, and great-grand-parents, eminent for zeal in the true religion.

"From William Fiske, a man of great intelligence and Christian integrity, descended a second William, who inherited largely his father's abilities and virtues. Ebenezer Fiske, son of William, junior, died at the age of ninety-two. The son of Ebenezer was born in 1786, and removed to Shelburne. He was a man of inflexible religious principles, and exerted a great influence on the growing community. His wife was a woman of energy and eminent piety, and would frequently set apart whole days to pray that her children might be a godly seed, even unto the latest generation. In 1857 three hundred of the descendants of this praying mother were members of Christian Churches."—*The Children for Christ*, by Rev. Andrew Murray, p. 199.

While I am speaking about heredity, I cannot help drawing attention to the striking case of it which is presented by the story of Jacob. The chief characteristic of that patriarch was, in his youth, a love of gain and a shrewdness amounting often to cunning. This he inherited from his mother, who, as a maiden, agreed to leave her father's home, and go with Eleazar to an unknown husband, when she saw the jewels of silver, and jewels of gold, and raiment which he had brought as a gift to his young master's bride. She it was who prompted him to play a disgraceful trick on her confiding husband. Her brother Laban and Jacob took the greatest delight in outwitting each other. Jacob stamped his own peculiarities on the Jewish nation, as witness the delightful story told by George Eliot in *Daniel Deronda*, about the little six-year-old Jacob Cohen, son of the pawnbroker, Ezra Cohen, who, after ascertaining that Daniel possessed a fine new pocket-knife, held out his own old worthless one and said with engaging frankness, "I'll shwop."[1]

Joseph is quite another type of Israelite—of those, and they are not a few, in whom there is no guile. We note that Joseph was the only one of the twelve patriarchs who was personally brought up by Rachel. Surely this leads us to the conclusion that, although not altogether free from the family failing, she probably attracted Jacob, and kept his undying conjugal love, by the beauty of her character as well as by that of her face. These remarkably human touches

[1] *Daniel Deronda*, vol. ii. p. 354.

in the Biblical narrative make us feel that we are dealing with a story of real life, and not merely with the history of tribes. Ancient history has given us a parallel to this, about 700 years later, in the tale of Troy ; and surely Dr Schliemann's researches have proved, once for all, that the family of Agamemnon were actual people.

Ecclesiastes i. 7

"*All the rivers run into the sea ; yet the sea is not full ; unto the place whither the rivers go, thither they go again* (or, *thither they return to go*)."

"It is from the ocean that all rain is primarily, by process of evaporation, derived. Clouds are masses of aqueous vapour, drawn in greatest abundance from those regions where a heated atmosphere, acting upon the expanse of water beneath, most facilitate evaporation—that is, from the regions of tropical heat. . . . The aqueous vapour becomes re-converted into water or, in very low temperatures, into snow or hail."—W. Hughes, *Class-book of Physical Geography*, p. 189.

Daniel iv. 28–30

"*All this came upon the King Nebuchaanezzar. At the end of twelve months he was walking in the royal palace of Babylon. The king spake and said, Is not this great Babylon, which I have built for the royal dwelling-place, by the might of my power, and for the glory of my majesty?*"

"In 689 B.C. the walls, temples, and palaces of Babylon were razed to the ground, and the rubbish thrown into Anakhtu, the canal which bordered the earlier Babylon on the south.

"With the recovery of Babylonian independence, under Nabo-polassar, a new era of architectural activity set in, and his son Nebuchadrezzar made Babylon one of the wonders of the ancient world."—Professor Sayce on "Babylon," in the *Encyclopædia Britannica*, Eleventh Edition.

Luke x. 17

"*And the seventy returned with joy, saying, Lord, even the devils* (or *demons*) *are subject to us in Thy name.*"

"It is told of her (Mary Magdalene) that she was delivered from that demon-possession which was then so prevalent in Judæa, and which, as Dr Nevius shows, is still seen in China.

"The native teachers in China say to the possessed, 'If you want to be set free from these tyrants of your spirits, cast out all idols from heart and home, read what Jesus and His apostles teach us, and pray to Him for deliverance.' And the cure works, for men and women who have been tormented for years by such demons arrive at deliverance and peace."—*Sunday School Times*, 23rd March 1913, p. 153.

1 *Timothy vi.* 15, 16

"*The King of kings, and Lord of lords; who only hath immortality, dwelling in the light which no man can approach unto, whom no man hath seen or can see: to whom be honour and power everlasting. Amen.*"

"The heat and light daily lavished by the sun would suffice to warm and to illuminate two thousand million globes, each as great as the earth."—Sir Robert Ball, *The Earth's Beginning*, p. 77.

"The brightest known star is 20,000 times as bright as the sun."—Sir David Gill at the Royal Institution.

2 *Peter iii.* 10

"*But the day of the Lord shall come as a thief; in the which the heavens shall pass away with a great noise, and the elements*[1] *shall be dissolved with fervent heat, and the earth and the works that are therein shall be burned up.*"

"That the earth's beginning has been substantially in accordance with the Great Nebular Theory is, I believe, now very generally admitted."—Sir Robert Ball, *The Earth's Beginning*, p. 368.

"We have pointed out the high probability that among the millions and millions of bodies in the universe, it may now and then happen that a collision takes place. Have we not also explained how the heat generated in virtue of such a collision might be sufficient, and indeed

[1] Heavenly bodies.

much more than sufficient, to raise the masses of the two colliding bodies to a state of vivid incandescence ? A collision affords the simplest explanation of the sudden outbreak of the star *Nova Persei* (Feb. 1901), and also accounts for the remarkable spectrum which the star exhibits." —*Ibid.*, p. 360.

Other cases of agreement between Natural Science and the Bible may easily be found, I think, in the works of modern archæologists.

www.ingramcontent.com/pod-product-compliance
Lightning Source LLC
LaVergne TN
LVHW050623100826
845148LV00011B/1712

* 9 7 8 1 5 9 7 5 2 2 8 5 4 *